NICHOLAS ANTHONY

DIGITAL CURRENCY

OR DIGITAL CONTROL?

DECODING CBDC AND THE FUTURE OF MONEY

ISBN: 978-1-964524-38-2
eBook ISBN: 978-1-964524-39-9

Printed in the United States of America.

Cover design: Roshni Ashar

Cato Institute
1000 Massachusetts Ave. NW
Washington, DC 20001
www.cato.org

CONTENTS

ILLUSTRATIONS

TABLES

FIGURES

ACKNOWLEDGMENTS

Many people have helped me both in my career and in the creation of this book. However, a handful of folks deserve individual thanks. For giving me the space to work and for making this project possible, I thank Norbert Michel. From my first blog post to now my first book, Norbert has only been supportive. For encouraging the development of this book in the first place, I thank Kevin Dowd. It was his urging that initially lit the fire for this project. For listening to countless readings and rereadings, I thank Sierra Kolasa for supporting this project and all my other endeavors. Were it not for her support, this project and many others would not have been possible.

For helping me come up with a title that somehow balanced the mouthful that is "central bank digital currency" with a focused hook, I thank Ann Rulon. For helping me think through the different concepts covered in this book, I thank Jordan Brewer, Jim Dorn, Tim Hite, Haakon Santaella, George Selgin, and Mariana Trujillo. For assistance at varying stages of this book, I thank Shota Natenadze and Nick Thielman. For help cleaning up the text and making sure my arguments were presented clearly, I thank Ivan Osorio, Joanne Platt, and Sara Proehl. And for guiding the book's publication, I thank Eleanor O'Connor.

I'd also like to thank everyone at the Cato Institute who has helped me along the way. From the front desk to the leadership team, everyone has been a joy to work with over the years. It is a true blessing to be surrounded by so many good people.

Finally, I thank Howie Baetjer Jr. for helping me discover my passion for research during my undergraduate studies. My career in economics would not have been possible had it not been for his guidance. The lessons Howie taught me both inside and outside the classroom have helped shape everything I've accomplished over the years.

1

INTRODUCTION

Central bank digital currencies, or CBDCs, are on the rise. In an attempt to reinvent money as we know it, central bankers and other policymakers around the world are currently researching, developing, and launching CBDCs.[1] However, there should be no misunderstanding: efforts in the United States and abroad are little more than a bid to solidify government control over money and payments.

That should be no surprise considering that the rise of CBDCs began after the rise of cryptocurrency. In fact, as this book will later discuss, it was the announcement by Meta (formerly known as Facebook) of its cryptocurrency Libra in the summer of 2019 that sent government officials into a frenzy. Panicked, many officials latched on to the idea that the government needed to launch its own version of cryptocurrency.

Yet a CBDC is not a cryptocurrency at all. In fact, in almost all the characteristics that really matter, CBDCs are nearly the opposite of cryptocurrencies (Table 1.1). Where Bitcoin was developed to be a decentralized system provided by the market, a CBDC would be a centralized

Table 1.1: Central bank digital currency (CBDC) and Bitcoin are near opposites

CBDC	*Bitcoin*
• Centralized	• Decentralized
• Government provided	• Market provided
• Closed and permissioned system	• Open and permissionless system
• Censorable	• Censorship resistant
• Unclear and discretionary monetary policy	• Clear and rules–based monetary policy
• Unlimited supply	• Fixed supply

system controlled by the government. Where Bitcoin is open and permissionless, a CBDC would be closed and permissioned. Where Bitcoin has clear rules and limits, a CBDC would be left to the discretion of the government.

Former Treasury Department officials Alex J. Pollock and Howard Adler have described this clash of principles as a great irony considering that "cryptocurrency was created because people were afraid of government control and wished to insulate their financial lives from monetary manipulation by central banks."[2] In contrast, "With CBDCs, their ideas would be used to increase exactly the type of government interference and control that the crypto creators sought to escape."[3] Pollock and Adler couldn't be more right. The increase in government interference and control that they describe is precisely the problem presented by the rise of CBDCs, and why CBDCs have become a much bigger issue than an overreaction to cryptocurrency alone.

In fact, this moment in time may very well prove to be an inflection point in monetary and financial history. A CBDC could even become the most significant development in monetary and financial policy since the creation of the nation's central bank—the Federal Reserve—just over 100 years ago. Where the creation of the Federal Reserve marked the end of competition in money in the United States, the creation of a CBDC could mark far worse. Put simply, CBDCs jeopardize financial privacy, freedom, and markets. Worst of all, there are no unique benefits created by CBDCs to justify those risks.

The idea of reinventing money through the creation of a CBDC has caught the attention of the president, Congress, international institutions, and government contractors, but the public has largely been left out of the policy debate.[4] When the Cato Institute surveyed a representative sample of 2,000 Americans in 2023, 49 percent of respondents said they simply did not know enough about CBDCs to support or oppose them.[5] That's where this book comes in. It contains everything you need to get up to speed on CBDCs so you can know the stakes before they are created. From the myths of CBDCs' benefits to the threats posed by CBDCs' risks, this book will help decode what "CBDC" means for the future of money.

2

WHAT IS A CBDC?

"A CBDC isn't just 'a different form of money.'"
—*Norbert Michel, Cato Institute*[1]

Before this book can explain what CBDCs might mean for the future of money, it's important to have a firm and common understanding of what exactly a CBDC is and how it relates to the money that many people already use today. As we'll see, in some ways CBDCs could seem relatively innocuous (or downright unnecessary) because of how much they overlap with the existing financial system. Yet in other ways, CBDCs mark a radical departure from money as we know it.

CBDC 101

To begin, a CBDC is a digital national currency that is a direct liability of the central bank. In the United States, a CBDC would be a digital form of the U.S. dollar. Whereas elsewhere, for example, there is currently a CBDC that is a digital form of the Nigerian naira, referred to as the eNaira. However, a CBDC is much more than "just another form of money."[2] In practice, a CBDC's direct, digital liability status means that central banks can be directly connected to individual transactions—a radical deviation from how money currently works.[3] Hardly anyone asks, "Whose liability is it anyway?" when making or receiving a payment, yet in the case of CBDCs, that question is crucial.

It is true that a CBDC would be like cash, or paper money, insofar as both are a liability of the central bank; however, this characteristic does not amount to much in practice when it comes to cash. The analog nature of cash means that it is essentially disconnected from the central bank once it enters the market. Sure, the central bank maintains cash in that it will replace damaged bills—but even then, that's only when bills are identified as unfit for circulation after being deposited by commercial banks.[4] So currently, the central bank does not have a direct relationship with individuals or a direct hand in their exchanges. However, that condition changes when a CBDC is introduced because a CBDC would create a sort of digital tether between individuals and the central bank—allowing the central bank to fully surveil transactions, program payments, and seize money (all topics that will be addressed at length in later chapters).

To get a better sense of how a CBDC is a departure from the current system,[5] let's move away from thinking about cash to consider how digital money currently works in the private sector. As it stands, the idea of "digital money" isn't novel. People regularly send digital payments using credit cards, debit cards, prepaid cards, and several mobile applications (e.g., Zelle, PayPal, and Cash App).[6] Considering the simplest example, the balance on a prepaid debit card is a liability of the private company that issued it (e.g., Visa or Mastercard). Similarly, when consumers deposit money into their bank accounts, the deposits in those accounts are a liability of the bank (e.g., Bank of America or Capital One). In either case, that means the financial institution owes the customer the funds on the card or deposited in the account. When a customer transfers that money to make a payment, the financial institution that owns the liability is responsible for transferring the money.

In the case of a CBDC, however, the digital money would be a liability of the central bank itself. In other words, the government would have the direct responsibility to hold, transfer, or remit those funds to the ostensible owner. This feature creates a direct link between citizens and the central bank. And it is this feature that opens the door to concerns regarding financial privacy and freedom related to the rise of CBDCs.

However, while those issues will be described at length later in this book, let's briefly discuss a few of the different models that a CBDC might be introduced as.

CBDC Models

Now, don't worry. This book is not meant to be limited to economists or engineers. This section will be kept short to avoid going too deep within the weeds. Given that this book is meant to raise awareness about CBDCs, it would be a shame if I lost you in the second chapter! With that said, some technical details should be hashed out considering that CBDCs can come in a few forms.[7] That's right. As if "CBDC" wasn't enough to decode, there is also "rCBDC," "wCBDC," and "iCBDC" to consider. Let me explain.

Given that CBDCs are such a new endeavor for governments and so few have actually been launched, there are several core models for how one might be designed. Generally, these models are based on who will be using the CBDC: the general public, financial institutions, or both. In that sense, the conversation revolves around retail CBDCs for the public and wholesale CBDCs for financial institutions. However, in a blurring of the two models, there is also the idea of an intermediated CBDC. Let's consider each in turn.

A retail, or direct, CBDC would be meant primarily for the general public to use for everyday transactions. Generally speaking, most conversations about CBDCs tend to describe this model. A retail CBDC is meant to emulate the digital money that people already use to purchase goods, pay salaries, and store wealth. The difference is that rather than Bank of America, Visa, or PayPal managing the funds, the central bank will be the one to directly oversee everything.

The Reserve Bank of India described retail CBDCs saying, "In this model, the CBDC represents a direct claim on the central bank, which keeps a record of all balances and updates it with every transaction."[8] Although sweeping surveillance has long been considered a disadvantage in the eyes of citizens and civil liberties advocates,[9] the Reserve Bank of India went on to note that an "advantage" of a retail CBDC is that "the central bank has complete knowledge of retail account balances." On the other hand, though, the Reserve Bank of India noted that a disadvantage is that a retail CBDC "marginalizes private sector involvement and hinders innovation in the payment system," and warned that the retail CBDC "model is designed for disintermediation[,] has the potential to disrupt the current financial system[,] and will put [an] additional burden on the central banks in terms of managing customer on-boarding [as well as] KYC [know-your-customer] and AML [anti–money laundering] checks[—]which may prove difficult and costly to the central bank."[10] In short, a retail CBDC would be the most straightforward path for a CBDC to increase financial surveillance, government control over the payments system, and the risk of destabilizing the financial system. However, again, those are all issues that will be addressed at length in later chapters.

A wholesale CBDC, in contrast, would be restricted to financial institutions and only used as a tool for settling balances between those institutions. When testifying before the U.S. House Committee on Financial Services, Federal Reserve chair Jerome Powell described the idea saying, "It would look an awful lot like a bank reserve and you might ask, 'Why would we need it,' and that's a really good question."[11] In other words, wholesale CBDCs are unlikely to offer anything novel to the market because innovations are already taking place on this front.[12] This sentiment was later formalized in a paper by Federal Reserve researchers who found that creating a CBDC for financial institutions "is not itself a novel activity since [financial institutions] currently have access to central bank money in a digital form."[13] However, it's not just governments that have created wholesale payment options for financial institutions. Even the private sector has innovated in this space. So a wholesale CBDC seems to be, at best, too little too late.[14]

An intermediated CBDC offers sort of a mix between the retail and wholesale models.[15] It would be for direct use by the public, but the accounts—or digital wallets—in which the CBDC is held would be maintained by an intermediary, such as a bank or credit union. This idea is most likely an attempt to appease the private sector by *appearing* to lessen the risk of a retail CBDC disrupting, or disintermediating, the current financial system (issues we will dive into later in this book). For example, the Federal Reserve claims, "An intermediated model would facilitate the use of the private sector's existing privacy and identity-management frameworks; leverage the private sector's ability to innovate; and reduce the prospects for destabilizing disruptions to the well-functioning U.S. financial system."[16] While such a statement may seem to suggest this model would not undermine private markets, it's really an empty promise.[17] The private sector may maintain the accounts, but the CBDCs in those accounts would still be a direct liability of the central bank. More so, having traditional banks maintain CBDC accounts could actually heighten the risk of a bank run considering that, theoretically, moving one's deposits into a CBDC account could be done within the same banking apps that customers are already using. Just as important, the government could still keep a record of balances and have a direct hand in consumer affairs. So although this model may be an attempt to appease the private sector, the risks posed by the direct CBDC model are far from eliminated. In fact, the intermediated model really boils down to being a "retail CBDC with extra steps."

Table 2.1: CBDCs can come in a few different forms

	Issuer	*End user*	*Maintainer*
Retail CBDC	Central bank	General public	Central bank
Wholesale CBDC	Central bank	Financial institutions	Central bank
Intermediated CBDC	Central bank	General public	Central bank and financial institutions

Conclusion

In short, a CBDC can come in a few different forms, and new designs are likely to emerge as debates move forward and new technologies are developed (Table 2.1). But the general idea of digital money is far from novel. The only thing that a CBDC seems to be pioneering is the creation of a direct line from citizens to the central bank.

3

Cbdcs SERVE NO GOOD PURPOSE

*"What problem would a CBDC solve? Alternatively, what
market failure or inefficiency demands this specific intervention?
After careful consideration, I am not convinced as of yet that
a CBDC would solve any existing problem that is not being
addressed more promptly and efficiently by other initiatives."*
—*Christopher J. Waller, Federal Reserve Board of Governors*[1]

CBDCs have gained the attention of central bankers,
policymakers, academics, and even the tech industry,[2] but
what purpose would they serve? Would a CBDC actually
improve the economy for Americans rich and poor? What
exactly justifies reinventing a nation's money? Or maybe
more pointedly, what exactly justifies experimenting with
the money in hundreds of millions of pockets across the
country and across the globe?

Proponents have been quick to offer a near endless list
of possibilities.[3] And to be fair, many of those possibilities
sound quite nice. For example, proponents commonly promise that a CBDC would improve the progress of financial
inclusion, the efficiency of the payments system, and even
the effectiveness of monetary policy. In fact, some have even

argued that the U.S. dollar's status as the world's reserve currency can only be maintained by the United States adopting a CBDC. All these features are worthy goals, yet all these promises fail to stand up to scrutiny.

Let's take a tour of some of the promises that proponents have made to show how they fail in practice. As we will see, a CBDC is not the panacea many have made it out to be.

A CBDC for Financial Inclusion

Improving financial inclusion is a praiseworthy endeavor, but CBDC proposals have done little to address the actual needs of those on the outskirts of the financial system. While financial inclusion itself covers a vast array of issues, let's focus on the issue of unbanked and underbanked Americans. It may be surprising to hear, but there are about 5.9 million American households that are considered unbanked because they do not have access to a bank account.[4] An additional 18.7 million American households are considered underbanked because they do have access to a bank account, but they routinely choose alternatives such as payday lenders, check-cashing stores, and the like.[5] Proponents of CBDCs commonly promise that financial inclusion—or, as the saying goes, "banking the unbanked"—will naturally result from the creation of a CBDC, but the logic behind that assumption is far from sound.[6]

Let's begin by considering what drives Americans to be unbanked or underbanked. The Federal Deposit Insurance Corporation (FDIC) has routinely conducted surveys since 2009 to explore this question in detail. The FDIC's most recent survey found not only that 72 percent of the unbanked were simply uninterested in having a bank account

Figure 3.1: Interest in having a bank account among unbanked households

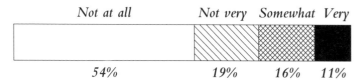

Not at all	Not very	Somewhat	Very
54%	19%	16%	11%

Source: Federal Deposit Insurance Corporation (FDIC), *FDIC National Survey of Unbanked and Underbanked Households* (Washington: FDIC, 2022).

(Figure 3.1), but also that the unbanked are so because of a number of specific reasons (Figure 3.2).[7]

The first reason that unbanked Americans commonly point to is that they do not have enough money to meet the minimum balance requirements to open a bank account.[8] At first glance, a CBDC might look like a solution, since the government could theoretically subsidize accounts to help depositors meet minimum balance requirements and even eliminate some maintenance fees on the front end. Yet there are several problems with this approach.

Subsidizing accounts might eliminate the costs for individuals initially, but there is nothing inherently unique about a CBDC that is needed to make that happen. It could be done with any of the existing options. The financial system does not need to be reinvented to effectively subsidize a prepaid card. And yet even if a CBDC account were to be subsidized, that wouldn't really "bank the unbanked." The problem is that a CBDC account and a bank account are not the same thing. Rather, a CBDC account would be more like a digital wallet. In this scenario, the unbanked would be no more banked than if the government simply put all their cash holdings onto, again, prepaid cards. A CBDC account

Figure 3.2: Reasons for not having a bank account among unbanked households in 2021

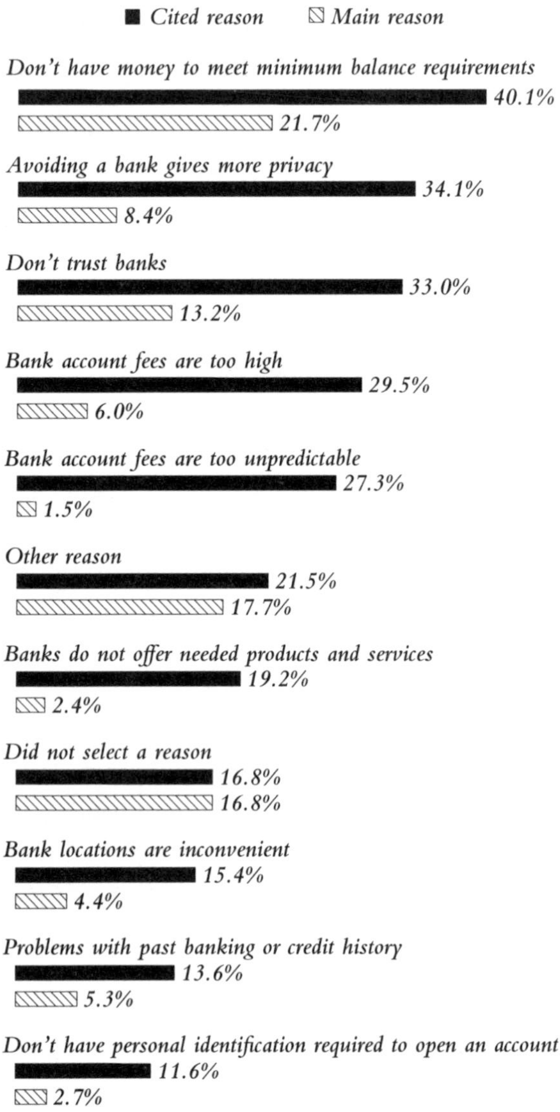

■ *Cited reason*   ◻ *Main reason*

Don't have money to meet minimum balance requirements
40.1%
21.7%

Avoiding a bank gives more privacy
34.1%
8.4%

Don't trust banks
33.0%
13.2%

Bank account fees are too high
29.5%
6.0%

Bank account fees are too unpredictable
27.3%
1.5%

Other reason
21.5%
17.7%

Banks do not offer needed products and services
19.2%
2.4%

Did not select a reason
16.8%
16.8%

Bank locations are inconvenient
15.4%
4.4%

Problems with past banking or credit history
13.6%
5.3%

Don't have personal identification required to open an account
11.6%
2.7%

Source: Federal Deposit Insurance Corporation (FDIC), *FDIC National Survey of Unbanked and Underbanked Households* (Washington: FDIC, 2022).

may offer *another option* for accessing digital dollars, but that's not the same as gaining access to financial services writ large (e.g., loans, credit cards, interest-bearing accounts, overdraft protection). Perhaps recognizing this fatal flaw, some have called for the government to also offer banking services through the United States Postal Service, but that is an issue with too many flaws to dive into here.[9]

The second reason commonly cited by the unbanked is a concern for privacy. To be clear, banks certainly do collect a great deal of information about their customers. One reason for this data collection is to establish a professional relationship with customers. It's hard to trust people to pay back their loans if you don't know where to find them and it's hard to judge how much they might be good for if you don't know their income. However, another reason is that banks are required by law to collect identifying information and routinely report that information to the federal government.[10] For example, one of the most infamous pieces of the modern financial system is the requirement for banks and other financial institutions to collect know-your-customer (KYC) information. This requirement was formally established by the Patriot Act of 2001, but it built on similar requirements in the Bank Secrecy Act of 1970.[11] Taken together, laws and regulations like these required banks to file more than 26 million reports on Americans for using their own money in 2022 alone.[12]

If history is any indication of what's to come, a CBDC would increase the current level of surveillance by offering the option of having financial activity on government databases by default—the exact opposite of a solution for privacy concerns. It is possible that a CBDC could win some favor if it were to have the same privacy features one can expect from cash, but many government officials have already ruled out the possibility of anonymity.[13] In fact,

officials have most commonly done so by noting that anonymity cannot be offered due to the "need" to comply with
know-your-customer and other Bank Secrecy Act requirements. So to the extent that unbanked and underbanked
Americans are concerned about privacy, it's unlikely that a
CBDC will be a solution. In fact, many unbanked Americans would likely go out of their way to avoid a CBDC.

The third reason—and the last one we will consider
here—is the concern about trust. Whether over concerns
about being treated fairly or concerns about one's money
being kept safe, many people avoid the banking system
because they simply do not trust it. One may be tempt-
ed to see a CBDC as an answer to this issue considering a
CBDC would be, by definition, another option for people.
Yet, there are a few problems with this thinking. Put simply, a CBDC is unlikely to help people who do not trust
the banks because, quite frankly, people don't really trust
the government either. As Pew Research has shown with its
collection of survey data over the past 60 years, the percentage of Americans who say they trust the U.S. government to
do what is right is at near record lows (Figure 3.3).[14]

Unless the U.S. government can turn this trend around,
it is unlikely that Americans will trust it with their money. In
fact, a 2023 survey by the Cato Institute found that 85 percent of Americans would prefer to keep their money in a
private bank rather than with the government.[15] Given the
U.S. government's recent attempts to surveil bank accounts
with as little as $600 of annual activity and the revelation
that more than 6 million records were collected on money
transfers without a warrant, it's unlikely the government is
going to gain Americans' financial trust anytime soon.[16]

Before moving on to the next benefit that CBDC proponents often promise, let's set aside what's been said thus far

Figure 3.3: People who say they trust the U.S. government to do what is right

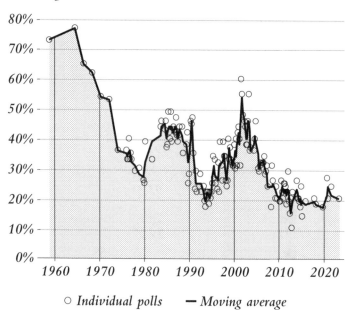

○ *Individual polls*   — *Moving average*

Source: "Public Trust in Government: 1958–2022," Pew Research Center, June 6, 2022.

for a moment. Let's even assume a CBDC is exactly what unbanked and underbanked Americans want. Even then, there's still another reason that a CBDC is unlikely to be helpful in practice—namely, there are fewer unbanked Americans every year (Figure 3.4). Since 2011, the percentage of unbanked households has been cut almost in half. This progress is important for our understanding because it could take upward of 10 years for a U.S. CBDC to be developed.[17] To put the timeline into perspective, China began its CBDC research around 2014 and only started its CBDC pilot in 2020.[18] Four years later, China's CBDC has yet to be used by more than 10 percent of the population.[19] By the time the U.S. government

Figure 3.4: Unbanked households in the United States over time, 2011–2021

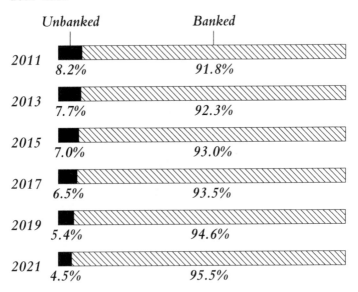

Source: Federal Deposit Insurance Corporation (FDIC), *FDIC National Survey of Unbanked and Underbanked Households* (Washington: FDIC, 2022).

introduces a CBDC, the number of unbanked households may be down to only those that prefer to remain unbanked.[20]

So, in short, there is no reason to launch a CBDC if the goal is to subsidize accounts. Even then, having a CBDC account is not the same as having a bank account or access to broader financial services. Worse yet, a CBDC may not even be used, considering that many unbanked Americans avoid the banks to preserve their privacy. In fact, even if privacy protections could somehow be sufficiently ingrained,[21] the unbanked may still not trust it given the general perception of the government and the government's long-standing encroachment on financial privacy. Taken together, a CBDC is no solution for financial inclusion.

A CBDC for Faster Payments

Just as it often surprises people to learn how many Americans do not have bank accounts, it often surprises people when they learn how the U.S. payments system has lagged behind other nations with regard to payment speeds. It may appear fast at first glance; however, in reality the U.S. payments system has long seemed, in the words of George Selgin of the Cato Institute and Aaron Klein of the Brookings Institution, "more like it belongs to a developing nation than to one of the wealthiest countries on the planet."[22] To be clear, initiating a transaction can take seconds. The problem comes during settlement—a process that can take days. It is here that proponents often promise that faster payments can be achieved with CBDCs.[23] The problem is that they offer too little too late.

In a 2021 report, Douglas Elliott and Larissa de Lima of the consultancy Oliver Wyman offer a sound warning for policymakers: do not make the mistake of ignoring alternative policy tools that might be better suited for the problems at hand.[24] Policymakers often make the mistake of thinking that central banks have unlimited funding, but that mistake should not be worsened by dedicating that funding to reinventing the wheel. As it stands, the United States already has four answers for improving the speed of the payments system: the Real-Time Payments (RTP)® Network, FedNow®, stablecoins, and Fedwire.[25]

Let's begin with the Real-Time Payments Network.[26] In 2017, a consortium of private banks finally put the United States on the faster-payments map with the launch of the Real-Time Payments Network—a system designed to offer instant settlements for payments between member institutions across the country.[27] Yet there is a challenge with this idea. Like new social media sites and even money itself, a network is only successful if it can gain enough users. To its credit, despite a slow start, the Real-Time Payments Network has steadily expanded since its 2017 launch, but it seems the Federal Reserve may have thrown a wrench in the engine with FedNow.

In 2019, the Federal Reserve announced that despite previously encouraging the development of the Real-Time Payments Network, it would introduce FedNow as its own solution—a platform that wasn't launched until the summer of 2023.[28] Critics were quick to point out that the Federal Reserve's intervention rested on a less-than-solid foundation.[29] Generally speaking, the only time the government should be able to justify an intervention in the market is when a clear market failure cannot be solved by private actors. Yet here, the slow payments problem was already being addressed by the Real-Time Payments Network. At best, the Federal Reserve's argument is that the network had not gained enough momentum in its first two years of operation, but that is hardly a sound justification for the intervention. Although officials may claim they were interested in promoting competition, the playing field tipped in its favor once the Federal Reserve announced its entry because of its privileged legal position as regulator, auditor, and now competitor. Still, even with those objections on the table, the fact remains: the U.S. economy now has at least two options for faster payments.

Another option has emerged from the private sector that has been gaining increased attention: stablecoins. More and more, stablecoins have been brought up in discussions about payments.[30] A stablecoin is a type of cryptocurrency whose value is tied to government currencies, short-term securities, or commodities. In practice, stablecoins have made the dollar more accessible than ever before by opening an entirely new way to transfer dollars for remittances, payments, and exchanges. However, it seems history may be repeating itself with this innovation. Although FedNow's interruption of the Real-Time Payments Network should be viewed as a cautionary tale, it appears that some are keen on repeating history by having the Federal Reserve interrupt the progress of stablecoins with the launch of a CBDC.

So far, we have walked (or perhaps sprinted) through the Real-Time Payments Network, FedNow, and stablecoins, where each presents a solution to faster payments from the perspectives of the traditional financial system, the federal government, and emerging finance. Yet there is still another option that could dramatically improve the payments space in the United States, and it predates stablecoins, FedNow, and the Real-Time Payments Network.

As George Selgin and Aaron Klein have explained at length, simply expanding the operating hours of Fedwire and the National Settlement Service could greatly improve the payments system.[31] This change would not lead to instant payments, but it would cut down on the days of delays caused by weekends and federal holidays—a big problem, as anyone waiting to gain access to recent deposits knows. This change alone would serve as a great improvement and cost very little. Yet for unknown reasons, the Federal Reserve has consistently tabled the suggestion. Despite the issue being brought up for years, Federal Reserve chair Jerome Powell said, "I'm not sure why we are not 24×7," when he was questioned before Congress in March 2023.[32] As it stands, all signs seem to suggest that the Federal Reserve preferred creating an entirely new system with FedNow over fixing problems within the existing system.

Considering there are so many options—both in the private and public sectors—it shouldn't be surprising to learn that even some government officials have questioned the need for a CBDC to achieve faster payments. For instance, Philip Lowe, governor of the Reserve Bank of Australia, said, "To date, though, we have not seen a strong public policy case to move [toward a CBDC], especially given Australia's efficient, fast, and convenient electronic payments system."[33] Elsewhere, Sopnendu Mohanty, chief fintech officer of the Monetary Authority of Singapore, said, "Every time we tried to find a problem statement that a CBDC is trying to solve, it seems to be that [our] faster payments system upgrade is solving for it already."[34] Even in the United States, Michelle Bowman, a member of the Board of Governors of the Federal Reserve System, said, "My expectation is that FedNow addresses the issues that some have raised about the need for a CBDC."[35]

In short, a CBDC offers no unique advantage to existing alternatives (even imperfect ones like FedNow). At best, the idea of introducing a CBDC to speed up payments is an idea that is simply offering too little too late. So again, it seems clear that a CBDC is really no solution for the payments system at all.

A CBDC for Monetary Policy

The promises of financial inclusion and faster payments are usually touted to draw in popular support for CBDCs, but there have also been similar attempts to win over policymakers with the promise of improving monetary policy implementation.[36] Still, they fall short.

The CBDC monetary policy story has several versions, but it often boils down to two core ideas: CBDCs will offer central banks the ability to use existing tools to fine-tune the economy at the individual level and CBDCs will open the door for new tools like negative interest rates. These concepts are often buried in the weeds among technicalities and jargon, so let's consider the ideas carefully to understand why a CBDC would not be the solution proponents promise.

When thinking about how monetary policy is decided, one might imagine rooms full of economists modeling potential outcomes and streams of data pouring down screens along the walls. In fact, one might even imagine something akin to the mission control center at a space shuttle launch. Yet a fundamental mistake can result from this thinking: the idea that monetary policy can set precise outcomes.

This mistake is most often seen in headlines when Federal Reserve officials meet to make decisions regarding interest rates. All too often, announcements come out that the Federal Reserve *set* interest rates at some amount.[37] As the emphasis might suggest, the mistake is suggesting the Federal Reserve sets the interest rate when what it really does is *target* interest rates—or more specifically, it targets the federal funds rate in the hope of influencing broader market rates. The Federal Reserve may be able to get rates near its target, but it has long struggled to reach and stay at its long-term goal of 2 percent inflation. Couple that reality with the understanding that monetary policy often involves long and variable lags, and it should start to become clear that "fine-tuning monetary policy" is a significant challenge. Take, for example, the experience in the 1970s or the 2010s. Both in times of rates being too high and rates being too low, the Federal Reserve has struggled to reach its policy targets. In fact, given the Federal Reserve's poor track record of managing the price level and business cycles, it is possible that it has undermined overall stability.[38]

Nonetheless, some argue that by tracking individual Americans' financial activity, the Federal Reserve could finally steer the economy in a positive direction. First, let's be clear about what's being proposed here. Financial surveillance might serve the government's interests, but it creates significant risks to financial freedom. Privacy, quite simply, is a cornerstone of freedom.[39] So this proposal is immediately a concern. Worse, it's unclear that such a strategy would work. Given how much the Federal Reserve has struggled to achieve its policy goals in the past, making changes directly to individual accounts could distort the market further. At least in the current system, banks have the capacity to act as a buffer when things go awry.

Moving on, what about negative interest rates? Is this tool the missing piece in the Federal Reserve's arsenal that a CBDC would unlock? Although CBDCs may be new, negative interest rate proposals are not. The basic idea is that much like how higher interest rates encourage people to *save* their money, a negative interest rate would encourage people instead to *spend* their money. In other words, negative interest rates would enable the government to "fine" everyone for not spending more. But what do negative interest rates have to do with monetary policy? If the economy was headed for a recession, the idea is that negative interest rates could be administered to stimulate spending and put the economy on a new growth trajectory.

Yet the idea of negative interest rates has additional costs that proponents often gloss over. The fact is that negative interest rates are only likely to be successful so long as people do not have access to alternatives. Options like foreign currencies, cryptocurrencies, and the like would all need to be banned for the proposal to truly succeed. Why? Because the success of the idea rides on people being spurred into saving or spending. However, if rates turn negative and someone does not want to buy anything, then an alternative currency could serve as an escape hatch.[40] Yet this escape hatch creates problems for the central bank. If people jump ship and abandon the dollar just as a recession sets in, it could prove more damaging than if people simply hunkered down with their savings.

To be fair, many economists and engineers have modeled the idea of fine-tuning monetary policy on the basis of individual transaction data and unlocking new frontiers with negative interest rate policy. Within the theoretical confines of those models, the findings are quite interesting. But when it comes to extending those models to applications in the real world, it's a much different story considering that these policies depend on an unrealistic expectation of knowledge, mass surveillance, and restricting the freedoms of real people.

With these factors in mind, it seems clear once again that a CBDC is really no solution for monetary policy.

A CBDC for the World Reserve Currency

As previously noted, proponents have promised a nearly endless list of potential benefits that could come from a CBDC.[41] But let's end with one promise that is unique to the United States: maintaining the dollar's status as the world's reserve currency. Unfortunately, like the other purported benefits described, strengthening the dollar is another case where the headline sounds good, but the substance is nowhere to be found.

A good question to start with is, "What makes the dollar the world's reserve currency?" First and foremost, the dollar owes its status to the strength of the American economy and the legal protections provided to private citizens. As Christopher Waller, a member of the Board of Governors of the Federal Reserve System, has explained, "The underlying reasons for why the dollar is the dominant currency have little to do with technology."[42] Yet for some reason, many people seem to overlook this reality. They see the rise of cryptocurrencies and foreign CBDCs as a threat from which America needs protection.[43]

To be clear, many countries around the world need to update their digital payments infrastructure. That one change, however, will not be the deciding factor for where their currencies stand on the world stage. For example, let's consider a few countries that have launched CBDCs: China, Nigeria, and The Bahamas.[44]

China's CBDC (the e-CNY) is unlikely to attract global demand considering the Chinese government's long history of violating property rights, financial privacy, and other human rights.[45] Who would volunteer to engage with such a regime? Businesses that depend on relationships with China may engage out of necessity, but it's unlikely that China's CBDC will earn global popularity otherwise. In fact, it may not even gain domestic popularity. Since being introduced in 2020, China's CBDC has struggled to gain significant adoption despite the Chinese government giving millions of dollars in CBDC handouts.[46] But let's set that aside and turn to Nigeria where there is a different set of concerns to consider.

Nigeria's CBDC (the eNaira) is also unlikely to attract global demand considering Nigeria's volatile inflation and tumultuous history.[47] Official inflation numbers have ranged

Figure 3.5: Nigeria's inflation has been too volatile for the naira to attract global demand

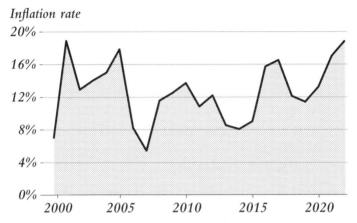

Inflation rate

Source: "Inflation, Consumer Prices (Annual %)—Nigeria," World Bank, accessed September 2023.

from 6 to 20 percent over recent years (Figure 3.5)—making it exceedingly difficult to invest in the naira and plan for the future. A CBDC does nothing to change that. And much like the experience in China, Nigeria's CBDC is even struggling to gain traction within its own borders.[48] Adoption only reached 6 percent after the central bank created a cash shortage in late 2022—a shortage so severe that it led to protests and riots in the streets.[49]

The Bahamas' CBDC (the Sand Dollar) is also unlikely to attract global demand. It has neither the severe human rights concerns of China nor the volatility of Nigeria. In fact, the Bahamian dollar is pegged to the value of the U.S. dollar. However, the problem here is that the Bahamian dollar doesn't have a wide enough network. For a currency to become a global reserve currency, it needs a substantial network of users so that acceptance is guaranteed nearly everywhere and at all times. For a country with a gross domestic product of $12 billion, it's unlikely to steer global markets—valued at $100 trillion.[50]

With these examples in mind, it should become clear that although CBDCs might be novel, they are unlikely to prove to be a deciding factor for a currency's success. There are simply far too many problems that require much deeper reforms. A CBDC is not going to fix a country's human rights violations, out-of-control inflation, or small size. Countries face unique challenges, which means that unique solutions are needed. There is no way a CBDC can fix everything everywhere all at once.

There is one last piece to consider regarding the dollar's role as the world's reserve currency. Although a CBDC is not a solution, it could become a problem for the dollar's world reserve status. As later chapters will explain at length, the risks to financial privacy, freedom, and markets that a U.S. CBDC would pose could lead people away from the dollar. For example, if a CBDC disrupts the banking system and increases the price of credit, it could undermine the strength of the U.S. economy. Likewise, if a CBDC creates greater financial controls, people might start looking into alternatives like cryptocurrency or foreign currency. But again, those are topics that will be explained at length later in this book. The point is that a CBDC isn't really a solution for the dollar's world reserve status.

Conclusion

Across the board, when it comes to the question "What is a CBDC good for?" the answer is clear: little to nothing. However, that's not the only takeaway here. It might be helpful to remind you of the title of this chapter: "CBDCs

Serve No Good Purpose." There is a reason it says, "no good purpose" rather than "no purpose." Although it seems CBDCs will provide little to nothing for citizens, they would provide expansive powers for governments. As we will discuss in the following chapters, CBDCs pose a foundational threat to financial privacy, freedom, and markets by providing government authorities unprecedented access into the lives of citizens.

4

CBDCs WILL END FINANCIAL PRIVACY

*"Freedom of thought, expression, and action are key to
unlocking each person's unique potential to contribute to
society. Untargeted government surveillance programs, even
well-intentioned ones, threaten that freedom."*
—Hester Peirce, Securities and Exchange Commission[1]

Americans have a right to privacy that is protected by the
U.S. Constitution, but the right to *financial* privacy has been
chipped away for decades.[2] Laws designed to counter terrorism, catch money laundering, and collect taxes provide
the U.S. government with the ability to conduct sweeping
surveillance over financial information.[3] In fact, the present
system leaves so much to be desired that some commenters
have defended CBDCs on the grounds that governments
already have so much control over the present system that
a CBDC would have little to no meaningful effect.[4] However, such arguments miss two important points. First, a
CBDC could spell doom for what few protections remain.
Second, a CBDC would further entrench decades of financial surveillance that should be reformed, not expanded, in
the digital age.

The Dismal State of Financial Privacy Today

Before diving into more detail regarding the risk that CBDCs present, some context will likely be helpful because financial privacy in the United States is not what it seems. Although Americans are protected by the Fourth Amendment to the U.S. Constitution and financial transactions appear to be private, the truth is quite the opposite. As it stands, the Fourth Amendment to the U.S. Constitution states,

> The right of the people to be secure in their persons, houses, papers, and effects, against unreasonable searches and seizures, shall not be violated, and no Warrants shall issue, but upon probable cause, supported by Oath or affirmation, and particularly describing the place to be searched, and the persons or things to be seized.

While this language might sound like it applies to financial records, the protections offered here were dramatically reduced when the Supreme Court held that records maintained by a third party like a bank or credit union were not protected by the Fourth Amendment. In *United States v. Miller* (1976), the Court held, "The depositor takes the risk, in revealing his [or her] affairs to another, that the information will be conveyed by that person to the Government."[5] This decision came to be known as the "third-party doctrine." Coupled with an earlier piece of legislation known as the Bank Secrecy Act,[6] the third-party doctrine gave way to the sweeping financial surveillance that is still seen today.[7]

The list of surveillance efforts that can be traced back to the Bank Secrecy Act and third-party doctrine is too long to draw out in full within these pages.[8] However, there are a few examples that are worth mentioning to illustrate the full scope of the issue.

Over the years, there has been no shortage of legislation to increase the scope of financial surveillance. Most notably, however, the Patriot Act and a $600 reporting proposal in 2021 showcase some of the key themes. The Patriot Act was a response to the terrorist attacks of September 11, 2001. Of course, stopping terrorism is a worthwhile endeavor, but the law dramatically reduced financial privacy in the United States in its effort to identify and thwart terrorist financing.[9] For example, the law introduced new requirements for banks to identify customers, expanded the reports banks are required to file on those customers, and prohibited banks from notifying customers when those reports are filed.[10] As if that were not enough, 20 years later, Congress pushed forward a proposal to monitor every bank account with at least $600 in annual activity.[11] The final version passed was slightly limited, but what's most telling is how the Treasury Department defended the proposal after public outrage swept the nation: "In reality, many financial accounts are already reported on to the IRS, including every bank account that earns at least $10 in interest. And for American workers, much more detailed information reporting exists on wage, salary, and investment income."[12] While true, the Treasury Department's statement reveals the dismal state of financial privacy in the United States.

Law enforcement has also increased their surveillance efforts. Between 2019 and 2022, U.S. Immigration and Customs Enforcement collected millions of records without so much as a warrant.[13] Matthew Guariglia, a policy analyst at the Electronic Frontier Foundation, described the surveillance saying, "This is a blatantly illegal exploitation of the government subpoena power—and an all too familiar one that must stop."[14]

Were legislated expansions and law enforcement investigations not enough on their own, inflation also has a part to play in increasing the level of financial surveillance. Because the Bank Secrecy Act's reporting thresholds were not crafted with an adjustment for inflation, each year with a positive inflation rate—which is most years—a wider net is extended for authorities to cast. For example, the reporting threshold for currency transaction reports (CTRs) remains at the same $10,000 level today at which it was set in 1972—a relatively large amount for a transaction in the 1970s.[15] Yet, if adjusted for the inflation that has occurred over the past 50 years, the threshold should be over $75,000 today (Figure 4.1).

So it is correct that financial privacy is already in a dismal state. Sweeping legislation, legal investigations, and even inflation have all steadily decreased the amount of

Figure 4.1: Inflation has steadily increased, but the threshold for currency transaction reports has never been adjusted

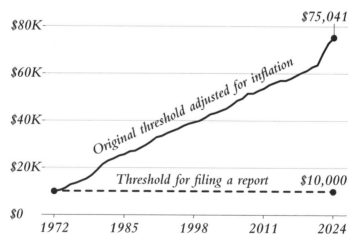

Source: Author's calculations based on data from Bureau of Labor Statistics, "Consumer Price Index (CPI) Databases," U.S. Department of Labor.

financial privacy in the United States. Yet, that is no reason to roll over and accept another heavy hit. Instead, substantial reforms are needed to bring the reality of financial privacy in the United States today in line with the spirit of the U.S. Constitution.[16]

A CBDC Would Only Worsen the Trend

Despite how troubling the current system is, introducing a CBDC could very well mean the end of what little protection for financial privacy is left. The third-party intermediaries that currently exist (e.g., banks, credit unions, payment apps) create a sort of air gap between the government and the general public. Government officials must find the right financial institution, coordinate with compliance departments, and check the appropriate paperwork if they are to see a person's financial activity.[17] It is not great and it is definitely not ideal, but this buffer really is the last stand between what little financial privacy exists today and complete financial surveillance.

A CBDC could spell doom for that last remaining buffer of protection because it would offer the federal government, as cryptocurrency industry experts Dante Disparte and Marta Belcher have warned, a "backdoor directly into your bank account" and "the ability to have absolute visibility into financial transactions."[18] In fact, the Federal Reserve has largely confirmed as much. Federal Reserve chair Jerome Powell told Congress in 2019, "If it is designed to be financially transparent and provide safeguards against illicit activity, a general purpose CBDC could conceivably require the Federal Reserve to keep a running record of all payment data using the digital currency—a stark difference from cash, for instance—and something that raises issues related to data privacy and information security."[19] In other words, a CBDC would establish a direct link between the government and citizens' financial activity. Rather than only having direct access to, for example, the more than 26 million reports that banks file and the 6 million reports that Immigration and Customs Enforcement collected,[20] the government would have direct access to everything, and that access would be by default.

Put simply, a CBDC would most likely be the single-largest assault to financial privacy since the creation of the Bank Secrecy Act and the establishment of the third-party doctrine.[21] Where the Bank Secrecy Act required banks to report on customers under specific circumstances, a CBDC would allow direct surveillance at all times. Where the third-party doctrine eliminated constitutional protections for information shared with banks, a CBDC would store financial information with the government by default.

The digital age has ushered in an unprecedented period of data collection, which means it's time to rethink the way financial privacy is treated, not further entrench the ever-expanding surveillance status quo. As explained by Supreme Court justice Sonia Sotomayor in a concurring opinion in *United States v. Jones*:

> More fundamentally, it may be necessary to reconsider the premise that an individual has no reasonable expectation of privacy in information voluntarily disclosed to third parties. This approach is ill suited to the digital age, in which people reveal a great deal of information about themselves to third parties in the course of carrying out mundane tasks.[22]

Justice Sotomayor is correct. This practice is ill-suited for the digital age and should be abandoned, not expanded.

Financial records offer far too much information about a person—a reality that was even recognized in the 1970s.[23] One might hope that the data would merely sit untouched, but history has shown that is unlikely. Time and time again, governments have used the financial system as a tool of control.[24] Aside from individual targeting, governments will likely look for "creative ways" to make use of the massive investment a CBDC would entail. Fishing expeditions, IRS audits, and political targeting could reach an unprecedented level.

A Wolf in Sheep's Clothing

In what is somewhat of a surprise, there have been recent efforts to propose "privacy-minded CBDCs." The idea is a welcome change of pace, but one that is likely too good to be true. There are several examples of proponents and commentators countering the concerns of CBDC surveillance by saying things like, "It just needs to be designed right" or "We just need a CBDC bill of rights." After reading this chapter and considering the history of financial surveillance (Figure 4.2),[25] the problems with these arguments are probably readily apparent. But to put things bluntly so it is abundantly clear: there is little reason to trust the government to establish a "CBDC bill of rights" when it has already done so much to undermine the existing Bill of Rights. From the creation of the third-party doctrine to the failure to adjust reporting thresholds for inflation, the government has largely eroded any protections for financial privacy.[26]

Another example from history might make the risk of proposing a privacy-minded CBDC more tangible. When Edward Snowden, a former National Security Agency (NSA) consultant turned whistleblower, leaked classified

Figure 4.2: The U.S. government has continuously chipped away at financial privacy over the years

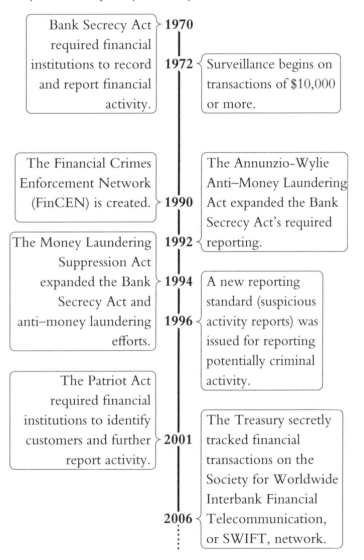

Figure 4.2: (*Continued*)

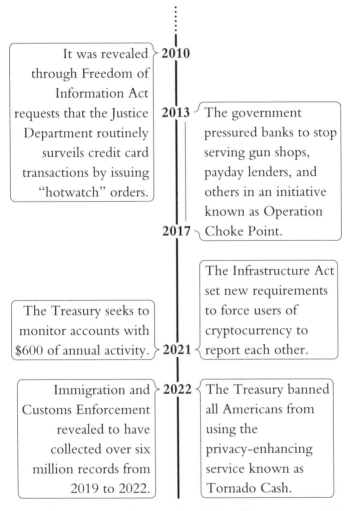

Note: This list is not exhaustive, but it does illustrate some of the key moments where the government has intruded on financial privacy.

information in 2013, it was revealed just how huge domestic surveillance had become in the wake of the September 11 attacks. Yet there was a smaller story within these revelations that is especially telling when considering proposals for a privacy-minded CBDC. Thomas A. Drake, a former NSA official turned whistleblower, shared how he proposed a system at the NSA that could have better protected the privacy of Americans during domestic surveillance.[27] The basic premise was that, although it would be a sweeping surveillance program, any identifying information would be anonymous by default. However, if there was actionable information, then a warrant could be secured to de-anonymize and identify to whom the information pertained. Drake took this proposal to NSA leadership, but he was ignored and eventually told that the NSA was not interested in the idea.[28] It later came to light that the program Drake proposed was used, but the section that would have protected Americans' privacy had been stripped out. In other words, the team that worked to create a limited surveillance system that would attempt to respect Americans' privacy inadvertently created one of the largest surveillance systems in U.S. history.[29]

This experience should be viewed as a cautionary tale for those seeking to promote CBDCs. Much like Drake's experience at the NSA, it's likely that even a well-intentioned design could quickly become something very different. Whether due to inertia or a crisis, the history of financial surveillance has already shown how something introduced subtly can quickly expand. Chris Meserole, director of the Artificial Intelligence and Emerging Technology Initiative at the Brookings Institution, put it well when he responded to a question about the risk of a CBDC being used for surveillance and control in the United States. "I'm not worried about the U.S. immediately

going down that road," he said, "but I do worry pretty significantly that once [a CBDC] is created, all it is going to take
is [an awful event such as a terror attack] and suddenly there
is going to be immense pressure to use that system in pursuit of different security or criminal justice activity."[30] Vitalik
Buterin, cofounder of Ethereum, has warned much the same,
saying that he once had hoped, perhaps naively, that CBDCs
could incorporate the transparency, verifiability, and privacy
of cryptocurrencies.[31] However, he said he has since found
that as CBDC systems are developed, the protections "all sort
of fall away."[32] Buterin described the failure: "We get systems
that are not actually much better than existing payment systems, because they just basically end up being different front
ends for the existing banking system. They end up being even
less private and basically break down all of the existing barri-
ers against both corporations and the government at the same
time."[33]

These concerns should not be shocking. Central bankers—
including Federal Reserve chair Jerome Powell, Bank for
International Settlements general manager Agustín Carstens,
European Central Bank president Christine Lagarde, and
Bank of England governor Andrew Bailey—have openly and
repeatedly said that anonymity and complete privacy would
not be an option with a CBDC.[34]

Given that the risks are so many, and the benefits are
so few, this path is one that is likely better left untraveled.
CBDCs are ill-suited for helping financial inclusion, too late
to improve payment speeds, unlikely to advance monetary
policy, and unhelpful for maintaining the dollar's world
reserve currency status. With that in mind, there should be
little doubt that governments most likely want CBDCs to
solidify their control over money in response to the rise of

cryptocurrencies. Likewise, there should be little doubt that organizations pushing CBDCs and tech companies developing them have a profit incentive to encourage CBDC adoption regardless of what they might lead to.[35] Therefore, proposals for a "privacy-minded CBDC" are, unfortunately, likely to prove to be little more than a wolf in sheep's clothing.

Conclusion

The threat to financial privacy posed by CBDCs has raised alarms as a leading concern across academia, industry, and even the government itself. "At some point, a CBDC that fails to provide a high degree of financial privacy will be used to monitor and censor the transactions of one's political enemies. It is foolish to think otherwise," noted economist William Luther of Florida Atlantic University.[36] Meanwhile, in a letter to the Federal Reserve Board of Governors, Deborah Matthews Phillips and Mickey Marshall of the Independent Community Bankers of America pointed out, "The creation of a CBDC will introduce significant privacy and cybersecurity risks into the nation's monetary system and disrupt the stability of America's banking system."[37] And in Congress, Rep. Andy Barr (R-KY), who sits on the Financial Services Committee, said, "The prospect of government surveillance of Americans' individual financial transactions through a CBDC and Fed accounts raises serious privacy concerns."[38]

Considering that the Bank Secrecy Act began in 1970 as a way to monitor foreign accounts and is now responsible for over 26 million reports on Americans a year, it should be no surprise that people are so worried about the threat a CBDC could pose to financial privacy.[39] There is little doubt that government officials will tout the risks of terrorists, drug cartels, and money launderers to justify the surveillance that a CBDC would bring. But there should be no misunderstanding that surveilling "for bad actors" also means surveilling innocent people. It's time to reduce financial surveillance, not further entrench it.

5

CBDCs WILL RESTRICT FREEDOM

"A key difference with a CBDC is that the central bank will have absolute control on the rules and regulations that will determine the use of the [CBDC]. And also, we will have the technology to enforce that."
—*Agustín Carstens, Bank for International Settlements*[1]

The threat to freedom that a CBDC might pose is deeply intertwined with its threat to financial privacy. Where financial data can reveal your relationships, profession, religion, political leanings, locations, and much more,[2] a CBDC would give governments a powerful tool to act on that information quickly and directly. Whether it's preemptive controls to take choices off the table, behavioral controls to nudge people's spending, or punitive controls to punish citizens, a CBDC would provide countless opportunities for governments to control citizens' financial transactions.

Prohibiting and Restricting Purchases

One way this control might take shape is through a CBDC with programmable controls designed to prohibit and restrict certain types of purchases. The design features that can be integrated into cash are largely limited to what can fit on the bill itself.[3] By contrast, the digital nature of a CBDC opens many new options that aren't limited by physical space. At first glance, many of these options might seem benign or beneficial. Yet even with the best of intentions, these controls are just a few steps away from serious abuses of power.

The idea of parents programming their children's lunch money to exclude sweets offers a simple illustration of the problem.[4] At first glance, the idea may seem to offer some promise—or at least for some parents that is. However, it's important to be mindful of the extended possibilities of such an option. The transition from parental controls to paternalist government policies would occur quite seamlessly with a CBDC.

Like a parent limiting sweets, a paternalist government might seek to limit, say, adults' alcohol consumption.[5] Although existing taxes already achieve similar effects,[6] a CBDC could offer a more direct strategy. For instance, rather than increase the cost of alcohol with a tax, governments could impose a direct limit on how many drinks a person could purchase in a night. Or to make matters more complex, the system could be designed to flag anyone who buys, for example, three or more drinks and paid for parking in an attempt to stop possible drunk drivers. These types of paternalist policies may sound appealing for some at first glance, but they can quickly fall apart in practice or lead to unintended consequences. For example, how would it account for someone buying a round of drinks for a group of friends? Or turning to more serious matters, what happens when those same controls are used to stop people from shopping at legal but politically controversial businesses?

For example, the issue gets worse when examining something like the legality of cannabis consumption. Currently, a troublesome clash exists between state and federal laws regarding the legality of consuming cannabis.[7] Many states have legalized cannabis, but federal law remains unchanged. In practice, this clash means that federally chartered financial institutions effectively cannot enter the market and take part in the profits even though they might operate in a state that legalized cannabis.[8] This issue is important to consider because it's hard to imagine how a CBDC could possibly be used to purchase cannabis so long as federal law remains unchanged.[9]

The lockdowns during the COVID-19 pandemic offer another example of how a CBDC could be used for targeted, preemptive controls. Police departments across the world expanded their staff and efforts to conduct lockdown patrols.[10] For example, in England, police caught an outdoor party with a few hundred people by using a drone.[11] In Spain, police used drones to issue warnings to those seen outdoors during the country's stay-at-home orders.[12] In Australia, soldiers joined police forces to knock on doors and make sure people were following the lockdown orders.[13] However, rather than have police walk (or fly over) the streets, a CBDC could have been programmed to allow transactions only with businesses deemed "essential." Or in the case of travel restrictions, a CBDC could freeze transactions and alert authorities of spending made outside an allowed travel radius.[14]

Although the cases thus far have been speculative, we can also turn to where CBDC advocates have already touted the control a CBDC could offer—albeit with more benign examples.[15] For example, Bo Li, deputy managing director of the International Monetary Fund (IMF), said in 2022: "CBDC can allow government agencies and private sector players to program . . . targeted policy functions. By programming a CBDC, money can be precisely targeted for what people can own and what [people can do.]"[16] To be fair, Li made this statement within the context of financial inclusion and food stamps. Yet if that is the sole focus of the controls he or the IMF had in mind, it's unclear why a CBDC is necessary considering that SNAP (Supplemental Nutrition Assistance Program) and EBT (Electronic Benefits Transfer) cards already do just that.[17] The only thing a CBDC is in a unique position to do is to expand the ability to apply these controls to everyone.

In short, while some proponents could have the best of intentions when they propose using the programmable nature of a CBDC—to protect citizens from themselves, expand the tools of law enforcement, and establish direct controls over the use of aid—it cannot go ignored that these same tools have the potential for misuse. Through either innocent mistakes or sinister motives, the ability to prohibit and restrict citizens' purchases at this scale offers too much power to governments.

Curbing and Spurring Spending

Beyond preemptive controls, a CBDC could also be used to establish controls to change consumer behavior. One approach is through the implementation of both positive and negative interest rates.[18] These rates could be used to curb and spur spending, respectively.[19]

The idea behind paying, and subtracting, interest on CBDCs largely boils down to controlling the demand for money. Just like how the demand for candy spikes as Halloween grows near, and falls back again after Halloween, so too can the demand for money change over time. In the extreme, hyperinflation has reduced the value of money to the point that there is so little demand that cash has been seen littered throughout the streets. In fact, hyperinflation is so extreme that it can even drive people to shift their demand to other types of money, such as foreign currency and even cryptocurrency.[20] The demand for money can also be observed in more subtle instances. Throughout history, there have been times when the demand for money fluctuates, such as when migrant farmers would "cash out" at the end of a harvest season.[21] So while it's true that the demand for money may not be as obvious as the demand for goods like food or cars, it is nonetheless an important phenomenon.

The importance of the demand for money is partly what has sparked interest in CBDCs for policymakers. Monetary policy has long struggled from long and variable lags so some have speculated that a CBDC could be a solution to achieve more direct changes. The theory goes that use of positive and negative interest rates could give officials the ability to directly target and control individual demand, and to do so in real time.

Let's start with more familiar territory: positive interest rates. If a CBDC's interest rate is positive, people will want to hold more of that CBDC for long periods of time to accumulate interest. If the interest rate is high enough, people might *only* want to hold that CBDC. In that sense, policymakers can use positive interest rates to curb consumer spending and spur saving.

From an individual's perspective, the idea is that if you are receiving high-interest payments, it wouldn't make sense to go buy a new computer or car today because waiting could help you receive enough interest to cover some of the cost later. In other words, holding the CBDC becomes an investment strategy. From a policymaker's perspective, the thinking is that increasing the interest rate would stop people from spending money before an economy overheats.

If the interest rate is negative, however, people will want to spend their CBDCs rather than hold them. In that instance, the negative interest rate almost acts as a fine, or tax, for not spending money. In that sense, policymakers can use negative interest rates to spur consumer spending and curb saving.

Here, the individual and policymaker perspectives are simply the inverse of what occurs with positive interest rates. From an individual's perspective, the idea is that if you are receiving negative interest payments (i.e., being fined for storing money), it would be better to go buy a new computer or car today because waiting could mean you lose money and can't afford the cost later. From a policymaker's perspective, the thinking is that lowering the interest rate toward and into negative territory (i.e., increasing the cost for holding money) would push people to spend more money before an economy falls into a recession.

In either case, the success of the rates depends on policymakers' ability to accurately fine-tune the economy without creating market distortions—a difficult prospect, to say the least.[22]

There may be another problem. Whereas a positive interest rate may lead people to adopt a CBDC (especially if the rate is higher than the market rate),[23] a negative interest rate would drive people away from that same CBDC. Therefore, implementing negative interest rates successfully depends on consumers having no alternative payment methods. In fact, this condition may be part of the reason why so many CBDCs around the world have been accompanied by varying bans on cryptocurrency.[24] Yet even if governments were to successfully remove third-party competitors from the market for payments, policymakers still wouldn't be able to effectively implement negative rates with CBDCs as long as people can still switch to cash.[25]

Freezing and Seizing Funds

The final aspect to consider here is that of governments freezing and seizing people's money. This issue—much like other issues related to financial privacy discussed in Chapter 4—is not new; however, the advent of CBDCs could magnify both the scale and frequency of these challenges.

Whether it be a whistleblower, a protestor, or a rival political candidate, many authoritarian governments respond to criticism with force. In China, for example, Jimmy Lai—entrepreneur, newspaper publisher, and recipient of the Cato Institute's 2023 Milton Friedman Prize for Advancing Liberty—became the target of government intimidation because of his long-held commitment to a free press and support for the pro-democracy protests in Hong Kong.[26] Less than a year after arresting Lai, the Hong Kong police froze both his personal finances and the finances of three companies linked to his newspaper, *Apple Daily*.[27] In Russia, the late Alexei Navalny, activist and founder of the Anti-Corruption Foundation, had a similar experience when Russian authorities froze his bank accounts.[28] The freeze began just days ahead of demonstrations that were planned to protest the exclusion of opposition candidates in a local election in Moscow.

Examples of governments turning to the financial system to exert control are not limited to overtly oppressive regimes like those in China or Russia, however. In Canada, for example, Prime Minister Justin Trudeau resorted to invoking the Emergencies Act for the first time in Canadian history to shut down protests over COVID-19 restrictions in 2022.[29] As donations began to flow in from around the world (many coming from the United States), Prime Minister Trudeau chose to freeze the bank accounts of protestors to restrict access to funding and cut the protestors off from society.[30]

The U.S. government has also been unable to resist the temptation to use the financial system as a means for social control. Perhaps in the most infamous example, Operation Choke Point was a Justice Department initiative to go after politically disfavored businesses (e.g., state-licensed cannabis dispensaries, payday lenders, pawnshops, or gun shops).[31] Coordinating with other federal agencies, the Justice Department pressured financial institutions to deny services to those lawful businesses to, as one official described it, "chok[e] them off from the very air they need to survive."[32]

Governments of all types thus recognize that the traditional financial system is an effective tool for control. More so, in a time when social media can be used to rally support from around the world, governments recognize that using the financial system does not generate significant backlash given its relatively hidden nature. Unlike when governments deploy riot police, there are no photos of an official striking a devastating blow to a protestor or tear gas filling the streets. Instead, the moment of impact is when victims receive a letter from the bank or an error message in an app to notify them that they no longer have access to their finances. And yet, it can halt people in their tracks all the same—effectively cutting them off from their local community and the world at large.[33] For the billions of people living under authoritarian regimes, or simply subject to ill-considered laws, the potential for abuse of the traditional financial system is all too real.

Yet freezing funds is only half the story. There is also the possibility of governments seizing people's money. The most infamous example in the United States is that of civil forfeiture—or what the Institute for Justice has labeled "one of the gravest abuses of power in the country today."[34] Briefly, civil forfeiture laws allow law enforcement to seize people's money if they consider someone having money to be suspicious.[35] The problem, however, is worse than just vague guidelines. There is a profit incentive for law enforcement to seize funds and other items; there are ways for law enforcement to get around what few restrictions are on the process; and there is little evidence needed to justify the seizure. Perhaps worst of all, victims are held guilty until proved innocent and are required to fight the government in court to get their property back.[36]

Far too many stories have emerged of Americans being forced to fight the government because law enforcement did not like how much money they had—or, perhaps liked it too much.[37] A 2014 *Washington Post* investigation documented what it described as "the spread of an aggressive brand of policing that has spurred the seizure of hundreds of millions of dollars in cash from motorists and others not charged with crimes."[38]

Like the issues with financial privacy, the risk that a CBDC poses here largely lies in its ability to establish a *direct* line between people and the government. For example, in Canada, Prime Minister Trudeau would not have needed to invoke the Emergencies Act to order banks to freeze the accounts of protestors if Canada had a CBDC. Rather, the move could have been done directly and far sooner had the accounts been kept on a government database. Likewise, in the example with the United States, police would not be limited to seizing only the funds they see when interacting with the public in person.

These may be extreme examples, but they are what many CBDC proponents refer to when they describe the "AML/ KYC/CFT" capabilities of a CBDC. Those initialisms are short for "anti–money laundering, know-your-customer, and countering the financing of terrorism."[39] Compliance in this context means identifying who you are, what you do for work, where you live, a complete record of all your transactions, and much more. And it is in both autocratic and relatively free countries that financial surveillance can quickly translate to financial control.[40]

Conclusion

Put simply, the possibilities for the programmability of a CBDC are nearly endless. And in all of them, even the best of intentions are just a few steps away from leading to serious abuses of power. Whether it be deciding what purchases are allowed, fining people to spur spending, or outright seizing assets, a CBDC offers too many possibilities for government control that would drastically limit the freedoms of Americans. Much like the erosion of financial privacy over the past 50 years, even if a CBDC is initially introduced with safeguards to limit such controls, it's unlikely that politicians and regulators would be able to resist the temptation to tear down those safeguards for long.[41]

6

Cbdcs WILL DESTABILIZE BANKS AND CRYPTOCURRENCIES

"The more the state 'plans,' the more difficult planning becomes for the individual."
—*F. A. Hayek, author of* The Road to Serfdom *and recipient of the 1974 Nobel Memorial Prize in Economic Sciences*[1]

CBDCs pose a significant risk to both the foundation and the future of the financial system. Today, banks, credit unions, and other financial institutions stand to lose as a CBDC could dry up funding and increase the cost of loans for everyone. Tomorrow, cryptocurrencies stand to lose as politicians around the world are already trying to use CBDCs to block the emergence of competing cryptocurrencies.

Even if policymakers wish to avoid or hedge this outcome, they can do little if they choose to move forward with a CBDC. For there is no getting around what William Luther, director of the American Institute for Economic Research's Sound Money Project, calls the "CBDC tradeoff."[2] Put simply, if a CBDC is to be made attractive enough for consumers to want to use it, it will lead to people leaving both existing and emerging finance.[3] Yet the alternative is making a CBDC that no one wants to use. In other words, the tradeoff is between a useful CBDC that undermines the market or a useless CBDC that is a waste of resources.

To better understand how this situation would take shape, let's consider how a CBDC would disrupt the banking system and then look at how CBDCs have emerged as a tool to combat the rise of cryptocurrency.

An Exodus from the Banks

The risk that a CBDC would disrupt the banking system is one of the more technical complications.[4] Often referred to as "bank disintermediation," this risk can be more commonly understood as causing a flight of deposits—that is, a bank run. The idea is that, by leveraging its legal privileges, the government will create a CBDC that the public prefers over holding money in a bank account.[5] In effect, the public will run to the bank to get their money out of their deposit accounts and transfer it to a CBDC account. Yet, the basic business model behind banking is one of using deposits to fund loans. Therefore, as the supply of deposits decreases, it will become costlier for banks to issue loans—leading many to shut down or merge with larger institutions—and costlier for consumers to acquire loans. In fact, the loss of deposits might make banking more expensive across the board for customers. As Megan Greene, senior fellow at the Harvard Kennedy School, explains: "To make up for the lost fees [from losing loans], banks might charge more for payment services and accounts. So much for a cheaper and more inclusive financial system."[6]

After reading page after page about all the serious civil liberties concerns raised so far in this book, it might be hard to imagine why anyone would use a CBDC in the first place.

Setting aside that many people are likely to be unaware of the risks,[7] CBDC proponents have put a few proposals on the table to spur adoption and use—namely, in the form of above-market interest rates and de facto unlimited insurance. To better understand how these proposals play out, let's consider two situations: a time of peaceful planning when markets are stable and a time of panic when a bank is collapsing.

During a period of financial stability, CBDCs are a tough sell. As explained in Chapter 3, CBDCs are not a unique or well-suited solution to much of anything. Evidence from Jamaica and Nigeria suggests that people are, at best, uninterested in the idea.[8] Therefore, in an effort to spur demand, some CBDC proponents have called for CBDCs to offer features like above-market interest rates.[9] For many people, the allure of above-market interest rates could make choosing to hold their money in a CBDC account a quick and economical decision. Of the two scenarios, this one would likely result in people slowly leaving banks as they learn of the higher rates available from CBDCs.

During a period of panic, a CBDC may not be as difficult to sell. Rather than lure in the public by paying above-market interest rates, the public might be swayed by the unlimited de facto insurance a CBDC would offer. Consider a basic bank run where customers lose faith in their bank for one reason or another (often due to bad news about the bank's finances or a full collapse) and, as the name suggests, run to the bank to withdraw all their money. In the past, that primarily meant people ran to get their money out in cash. Yet, as technology has improved, people began transferring their money to other banks digitally. As the Federal Reserve itself pointed out in 2022, a CBDC combines features from both experiences in a way that would make "runs on financial firms more likely and more severe."[10] In fact, that same year, Denmark's central bank noted, "A retail CBDC without restrictions will immediately increase the risk of systemic bank runs."[11] Like cash withdrawn from a bank, a CBDC is a final means of payment or base money. Holding either means that you no longer have to fear losing what you have if the bank run leads to a full collapse. Effectively, your money is 100 percent "insured" instead of only being insured up to $250,000 in the banking system. As with transferring money to another bank, a CBDC is fully digital so there's no need to worry about the time waiting in line, the amount of cash available in the vault, the difficulty in carrying cash, and the security risk of storing cash.

We don't have to rely on theory alone to understand these risks. CBDCs may be novel, but the ideas behind them are not. Both government bank accounts and the quest for higher interest rates have a long history in the United States. Let's start with the latter case, as it is the simpler of the two.

Some politicians have cried foul over the "interest rate gap" between what banks receive from the Federal Reserve and what customers receive from the banks.[12] Therefore, some argue that a CBDC is the perfect way to cut out the banks and let individuals earn interest on accounts held directly with the Federal Reserve. However, a CBDC isn't necessary for this idea at all. In 2017, Connecticut-based Narrow Bank tried to offer a novel business model in an attempt to bridge the interest rate gap. The basic idea was to take deposits, invest them in reserves at the Federal Reserve, and pass on the interest directly to the depositors. Yet, the proposal was ultimately rejected by the Federal Reserve.[13] What makes this decision so interesting for the present discussion is that some experts have speculated that the Federal Reserve's reasoning for rejecting the proposal was because the Narrow Bank's plan was "too safe" and would disrupt the existing banking system.[14] If that was truly the case, it's hard to imagine how a CBDC would not pose the same risk on a much greater scale.

Further back in U.S. history, important lessons can also be gained from the experience of government-provided "bank accounts." From 1911 to 1966, the U.S. Postal Savings System operated on the premise of the U.S. Postal Service offering "safe and convenient places for the deposit of savings at a comparatively low rate of interest."[15] That low rate of interest, however, was set in stone by Congress and later became *comparatively high* when market rates fell during the Great Depression—a period that coincided with a significant number of bank failures.[16] This instance appears to capture both risks at play. In addition to people leaving banks in pursuit of a higher return, people also moved their money to the Postal Savings System in response to announcements of local bank suspensions.[17] Data available from the time show that the amount of money deposited in the Postal Savings System had increased nearly eightfold from $154 million to $1.2 billion right as market rates fell below the Postal Savings System's rate and banks began to fail.[18]

So, in both the best and worst of times, a CBDC could significantly disrupt the financial system. Yet, some CBDC proponents are not ready to throw in the towel. Instead, they have proposed making CBDCs intentionally less attractive to discourage and limit their use in a bid to reduce the risk of disrupting the existing system.[19] For instance, the Federal Reserve and the European Central Bank have proposed not paying interest on CBDCs, limiting the amount of CBDC a person can hold, and limiting the amount of CBDC a person can transfer over time.[20]

These restrictions bring us back to what William Luther described as the "CBDC tradeoff."[21] On the one hand, a CBDC could pay interest, offer subsidized payments, and maybe even have tax benefits. These offerings would lead people to leave the banking system, but it would mean that the CBDC gains enough users to be deemed a success. On the other hand, a CBDC could pay no interest, have some low cap like $10,000, and restrict how many transactions people could make. In that case, people probably wouldn't leave their bank any time soon, but then the CBDC probably would not gain enough users to be considered a worthwhile effort.

In short, the tradeoff is between making something people will want at the expense of the larger financial system or making something no one will want at the expense of taxpayer resources. If these are the options when it comes to the CBDC tradeoff, the best choice is not to introduce a CBDC at all.

A Challenger to Alternatives

It's not just the traditional financial system that stands to lose. The rise of cryptocurrencies has been closely monitored by central bankers and other policymakers alike. Fearful that cryptocurrencies could pose a challenge to state monopolies on money, many governments have launched CBDC initiatives to combat their rise.[22]

Examples are widely available of the anti-cryptocurrency motivation for CBDCs. In 2013, the Chinese government began what would become an eight-year-long series of attacks on cryptocurrencies.[23] It started with a notice prohibiting banks from handling transactions related to bitcoin and escalated to a complete ban on cryptocurrency trading and mining in 2021. The final ban came not long after the Chinese government began to launch pilot studies for its own CBDC, the e-CNY. Also in 2021, a bill in the Indian Parliament sought to criminalize the ownership of cryptocurrencies and then launch a CBDC to fill the gap left by the prohibition.[24] The Nigerian government chose a similar path ahead of the launch of its own CBDC, the eNaira, issuing announcements to remind banks that they are prohibited from engaging with cryptocurrency.[25]

Even in the United States, some policymakers view CBDCs as a tool to prevent the rise of cryptocurrencies. That much was made abundantly clear during the summer of 2019 when the announcement of Libra catapulted CBDCs into being a core issue in monetary and financial policy debates.

For those unfamiliar, Libra, later renamed Diem, was a cryptocurrency proposed by Facebook, later renamed Meta. Facebook organized a consortium of companies to back what would be a cryptocurrency pegged to the U.S. dollar and backed by a collection of currencies. This type of cryptocurrency is known as a stablecoin because it seeks to harness the technological benefits of cryptocurrency while maintaining the stable value of some traditional currencies.

The project quickly made waves among policymakers. In June 2019, Rep. Brad Sherman (D-CA) described Libra as "a crypto currency platform . . . to meet the needs of drug dealers, human traffickers, tax evaders, and terrorists."[26] Then in October 2019, Sen. Sherrod Brown (D-OH) said, "Facebook is too big and too powerful, and it is unconscionable for financial companies to aid it in monopolizing our economic infrastructure."[27] In November 2019, Rep. Jesús García (D-IL) introduced the Keep Big Tech Out of Finance Act to prohibit large technology companies from offering financial services (e.g., cryptocurrencies).[28] During a 2020 congressional hearing, Sen. Mike Crapo (R-ID) said, "Nothing amplified [financial stability] concerns more than Facebook's announcement of the Libra project last year."[29]

While Washington's response was devastating for Libra and eventually led to its demise, policymakers became fixated on never letting this happen again.[30] As *Politico*'s Zachary Warmbrodt reported in October 2019, just a few months after the announcement of Libra, "Lawmakers and Federal Reserve officials are so concerned about Facebook's plans to launch a new digital currency that they're contemplating a novel response—having the central bank create a competitor."[31] That competitor was, of course, a CBDC. As illustrated in Figure 6.1, interest in CBDCs skyrocketed after Libra.

Figure 6.1: Interest in CBDCs exploded after Libra announcement

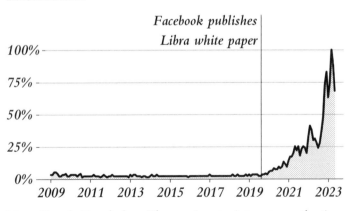

Note: Google Trends data. The y-axis notes interest over the time relative to the highest point.

To this day, "Libra" can still be heard echoing throughout the halls of Congress.[32] Even abroad, European Central Bank president Christine Lagarde said in May 2023: "The reason I'm personally convinced that we have to move ahead [with a CBDC] is a situation like the one we are in now. . . . I don't want Europe to be dependent on an unfriendly country's currency . . . or dependent on a friendly currency [that] is activated by a private corporate entity like, you know, Facebook or Google. . . . I don't want Meta, Google, or Amazon to suddenly come up with a currency that will take over the sovereignty of Europe."[33]

Conclusion

The introduction of a CBDC would severely undermine both the foundation of today's financial system and the future of tomorrow's system. Rather than choose between two bad outcomes in the "CBDC tradeoff," the answer should be not to issue a CBDC at all.[34]

7

CBDCs WILL WEAKEN CYBERSECURITY

"CBDC systems . . . could become an unimaginably alluring target for hackers—with potential disruptions even bigger than the shutdown of a crucial gasoline pipeline."
—David Z. Morris, CoinDesk[1]

Given the rise of hacks, ransomware, and data breaches in the digital age, it should come as no surprise that a CBDC presents a cybersecurity risk. A hint of the problem can be seen in its very name.[2] Centralizing data creates an attractive target for hackers, banks are known targets for hacks, digitizing information makes it available for hackers across the world, and currency is the goal of any profit-driven hack. Therefore, to launch a CBDC would be to put the nation's economy at greater risk of both hacks and system outages. Even organizations pushing for CBDCs recognize this risk. As noted by the Bank for International Settlements, a "CBDC system would be complex, with a large attack surface and many potential points of failure, bringing new and elevated risks."[3]

In fact, this risk was one of the earliest issues the Federal Reserve identified. Before later becoming a proponent of CBDCs, former Federal Reserve vice chair Lael Brainard warned in 2018 that "putting a central bank currency in digital form could make it a very attractive target for cyber-attacks by giving threat actors a prominent platform on which to focus their efforts."[4] In other words, to create a CBDC is to create a new set of cyber risks for the economy.

Hacks and Data Breaches

Given the long-standing recognition of the cybersecurity risk that a CBDC would create, CBDC proponents have already begun trying to develop ways to deal with the risks of hacks and data breaches. A 2023 Bank for International Settlements report on establishing CBDC security and resilience opens by noting that the report's advice rests on the assumption that "central banks have robust capabilities and practices for physical and cyber security."[5] But is this assumption sound?

Recent history has shown that the U.S. government is far from immune to hacks or data breaches. In fact, it seems financial regulators have been particularly troubled with safe-keeping the information they collect (Figure 7.1).[6] In 2023, the Consumer Financial Protection Bureau (CFPB) saw the data of 250,000 consumers exposed when an employee sent files to a personal email address.[7] After firing the employee, the CFPB reached out regarding the data, but the employee reportedly refused to delete the files when asked.[8] Then later in 2023, the Federal Reserve experienced a leak of confidential supervisory information pertaining to several banks.[9] In 2020, the Financial Crimes Enforcement Network (FinCEN) had more than 2,500 confidential, suspicious activity reports (SARs) leaked to *BuzzFeed News*.[10] In 2017, the Securities and Exchange Commission (SEC) revealed that its EDGAR (Electronic Data

Figure 7.1: The U.S. government has suffered many hacks and data breaches over the years

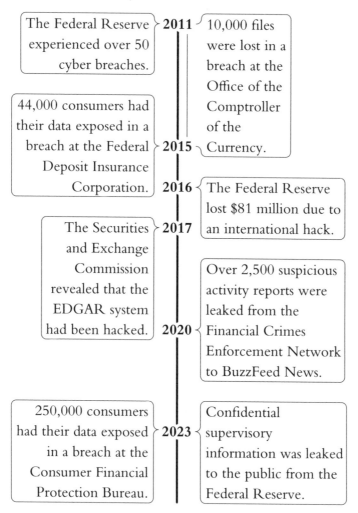

The Federal Reserve experienced over 50 cyber breaches.

2011 10,000 files were lost in a breach at the Office of the Comptroller of the Currency.

44,000 consumers had their data exposed in a breach at the Federal Deposit Insurance Corporation.

2015

2016 The Federal Reserve lost $81 million due to an international hack.

The Securities and Exchange Commission revealed that the EDGAR system had been hacked.

2017

2020 Over 2,500 suspicious activity reports were leaked from the Financial Crimes Enforcement Network to BuzzFeed News.

250,000 consumers had their data exposed in a breach at the Consumer Financial Protection Bureau.

2023 Confidential supervisory information was leaked to the public from the Federal Reserve.

Note. This list is not exhaustive and is limited to financial regulators.

Gathering, Analysis, and Retrieval) system—a comprehensive database of filings made by public companies and other financial firms regulated by the SEC—was hacked in the prior year.[11] In 2016, $81 million was siphoned out of the Federal Reserve after hackers broke into the system through the central bank of Bangladesh.[12] Also in 2016, the Federal Deposit Insurance Corporation (FDIC) experienced a breach when data for 44,000 FDIC customers was downloaded to a personal storage device by a retiring employee.[13] In 2015, an Office of the Comptroller of the Currency (OCC) employee downloaded 10,000 files to multiple thumb drives shortly before retiring. Notably, the OCC didn't notice the breach for nearly a year, and when it finally contacted the employee, the employee was "unable" to locate or return the thumb drives.[14] Finally, between 2011 and 2015, the Federal Reserve experienced more than 50 cyber breaches.[15] The list goes on, but the point should be clear: another hub of information in the form of a CBDC would make a significant target for hacks and a significant vulnerability for breaches.

To be fair, the private sector is no stranger to hacks. Plenty of financial institutions have been hacked recently.[16] However, the private sector has the unique advantage of being more decentralized than the federal government. For example, while an IRS breach would compromise the private financial data of 333 million Americans, a breach at a private financial institution would affect only a fraction of those citizens—leaving customers at other institutions free from harm. For example, Bank of America has approximately 67 million customers. Although that is a large number, it only represents about 20 percent of the American population.[17] This point is important to recognize because cyberattacks are a risk for everyone in the digital age. What changes are the incentives—the costs and benefits—for potential attackers.

To better understand the incentives at play, consider the case of decentralized cryptocurrencies like bitcoin. With a single bitcoin valued at tens of thousands of dollars, the bitcoin network might seem like an attractive target at first glance. However, the cost of attempting to hack it can quickly stack up.

A hacker may attempt to break into one computer in the system like hackers previously did to take $81 million from the Federal Reserve,[18] but the critical difference is that hacking one computer won't affect the bitcoin network. As a decentralized system, the bitcoin network does not hinge on any one computer.[19] Rather, there are countless computers around the world that work around the clock to verify the system. To hack the system itself, one would need to amass enough computing power to have a "majority vote" in what is known as a 51 percent attack. In other words, because the network is decentralized, someone can only seize control by acquiring at least 51 percent of the total computing power that is working to update the network.[20] Yet there are two costs to consider.

First, the level of computing power needed to achieve a 51 percent attack would be not only costly, but also massive and difficult to hide. There are currently industrial mining operations with entire warehouses of mining computers. Yet even those operations have not amassed 51 percent of the total computing power in the Bitcoin system.[21]

Second, such an attack might only work once—and even once might be questionable. Once the attack is recognized, others could choose to fork the system.[22] In other words, much like choosing which way to go when facing a fork in a path, a majority of users could decide to refuse to acknowledge transactions from what they identified as a clear attack on the system, and take a new path to return the network to its previous state. By carving a new path by forking the system back to its state before the attack, the bitcoins taken in a 51 percent attack could be rendered worthless.

Returning to the Federal Reserve and the case of a CBDC, the incentives change. Hackers would certainly face challenges with hacking a CBDC system housed at the Federal Reserve,[23] but that challenge is accompanied by a much greater reward. Compared with bitcoin's roughly $505 billion market cap, about $5 trillion worth of U.S. dollars are currently in circulation.[24] Yet the allure for hackers doesn't stop there. Hacking the CBDC system would also yield the financial records for every American. Considering that financial records would reveal people's profession, religion, location, relationships, and much more, they could be invaluable to hackers.

Other motives could be at play as well. A CBDC would also present an alluring target for hostile nations, hacktivist groups, and even spies. Given the complexity of U.S. relations across the globe, there is no shortage of possible contenders. Worse yet, as the Bank for International Settlements has acknowledged, these "nonfinancial motivations" could be particularly difficult to discourage.[25] Fending off these attacks is not as simple as making hacking attempts unprofitable.

Finally, it's not just outside threats that one must contend with. There are also insiders to consider. Whether they are foreign actors trying to infiltrate the Federal Reserve as employees to sabotage the system or employees seeking to leverage their access to defraud the system for financial gain, insiders pose a real threat.[26] In fact, the Federal Reserve already has a history with both concerns.

In 2022, a congressional report claimed, "China has recruited Federal Reserve economists for more than a decade to share sensitive and confidential information about U.S. economic policymaking in a bid to gain influence over the central bank."[27] To be clear, not all the employees identified in the report appeared to be complicit with the Chinese government. For example, in one instance, a Federal Reserve employee was detained four separate times by Chinese officials, who also threatened his family and tapped his phone.[28] Yet even then, this experience unfortunately illustrates one of the biggest problems with insiders: no matter how strong a cybersecurity system may be, the people in control remain a major vulnerability for centralized systems.

In 2021, the Federal Reserve became embroiled in a stock-trading scandal.[29] Although the story is complex, the general problem was that Federal Reserve officials are not supposed to trade stocks during certain periods if they have access to information about the Federal Reserve's upcoming policy decisions—the issue being that they could leverage that information to make profitable trades.[30] At the heart of the scandal, several officials with access to such information made trades that were highly questionable under the circumstances. Shortly after the scandal became public, the presidents of the Dallas and Boston Federal Reserve banks unexpectedly retired and the vice chair for supervision at the Federal Reserve Board stepped down.[31]

The true extent of the threats posed by China's efforts to infiltrate the Federal Reserve and Federal Reserve officials leveraging sensitive information for private gain is unclear. What is clear is that launching a CBDC would fly in the face of these warning signs. Whether in the extreme cases just described or something even as mundane as a disgruntled employee compromising the CBDC system, further centralizing the financial system risks creating an even greater target for hackers and an even greater risk of data breaches.

Outages, Too

Although perhaps not as concerning as a deliberate attack, system outages are a concern that has already started to emerge in practice with CBDCs.

The Eastern Caribbean's CBDC (DCash) experienced trouble early on when the system went offline in 2022. The Eastern Caribbean Central Bank—the central bank for members of the Eastern Caribbean Currency Union— quickly issued a public statement on January 14, 2022, to notify the public that it was aware that the system had crashed.[32] Even a momentary outage is a problem though. Reports later emerged that the system failed because of an expired certificate.[33] Although that might sound like a mundane technical issue, Pratik Savla, lead security engineer at the cybersecurity company Venafi, warned, "Not only can expired certificates cause unplanned system or service outages," but they can also "open the door through which malicious actors can find entry into one's environment."[34]

Fortunately, no public reports have suggested that the outage led to a hack. However, the good news ends there because this instance was not just a momentary outage. In fact, the outage didn't just last hours, days, or even weeks. It lasted months. The Eastern Caribbean's CBDC was down from January 14 to March 9, 2022.[35] Users effectively had their accounts frozen during this time with nothing but the Eastern Caribbean Central Bank's word that their money would become available when the system went back online.

The only silver lining with this experience was that it happened in a group of small island economies and adoption of the CBDC was low. If such an event were to happen in the United States or any other large economy, the results could be catastrophic. But before you say, "Well, it would never happen here," it's important to remember that outages have happened in the United States as well.

In 2021, the Federal Reserve experienced an outage for several hours.[36] Officials blamed the incident on an "operational error."[37] We may never learn whether an intern tripped over a power strip or a worker spilled coffee on a terminal, but what we can see is that even one of the most important central banks in the world is still vulnerable to small mistakes that can lead to major negative consequences. And again, we can see that further centralization of the financial system would make those negative consequences far worse.

Conclusion

Hacks, data breaches, and outages are serious risks for everyone in the digital age. There is no escaping it. Yet, that does not mean that people are powerless. When it comes to hacks and data breaches, it's important to recognize the incentives at play. Increasing the costs and decreasing the rewards for malicious actors means decentralizing processes and reducing information collection. Likewise, when it comes to outages, it's important to recognize that centralizing systems at a single point heightens the risk that human error, technological failures, and natural disasters could cause the entire system to fail.

To push forward with the launch of a CBDC is to ignore every one of these lessons.

8

CBDCs WILL JEOPARDIZE CENTRAL BANKS

"Moreover, we have yet to wrestle with the paradoxical possibility that CBDC may well increase the power and footprint of the central bank while also undermining its independence."
—*Christina Parajon Skinner, The Wharton School of the University of Pennsylvania*[1]

This book has covered how CBDCs could negatively affect individual citizens, the traditional and alternative financial industries, and the economy as a whole. However, there is another player that stands to lose from the rise of CBDCs: central banks.[2]

The suggestion likely seems strange. Central banks are pushing forward with CBDCs across the globe, CBDCs would give them a huge expansion of power, and the central bank for central banks (the Bank for International Settlements) has been a leading proponent of CBDCs. All signs seem to point to CBDCs being the greatest thing for central bankers since government monopolies. How could they stand to lose?

Quite simply, CBDCs risk both overwhelming and undermining central banks by forcing them to divert attention to customer services and become vulnerable to political pressures.

A Banker's Bank, Not a Commercial Bank

Opening the Federal Reserve's doors to all 333 million Americans would mean the Federal Reserve would need to drastically increase its workforce, its operations, and its ability to serve the public. To say this prospect would be overwhelming is an understatement.

To begin, the Board of Governors of the Federal Reserve System currently employs about 3,000 people and the 12 regional Federal Reserve banks (along with their branches) employ about 19,000 people.[3] At over 22,000 employees, the Federal Reserve System certainly has a large workforce.[4] However, these numbers pale in comparison with the nation's leading banks (Figure 8.1).[5] JPMorgan Chase, Wells Fargo, and Bank of America each have 200,000 to 300,000 employees.

With that said, using the employee head count for these banks does not offer an entirely accurate depiction of just how challenging serving the American public would be. Each of these banks serves only a fraction of the public. In contrast, offering a CBDC would mean doing business with *all* of the American public. Therefore, the Federal Reserve would need not only to meet the size of these private-sector banks, but also to surpass them.

Even if the Federal Reserve could pull off such a hiring marathon, there are other troubles to contend with. The Federal Reserve would need to then organize those employees within specialized departments. For example, Harvard Kennedy School senior fellow Megan Greene warns that issuing a

Figure 8.1: Major banks' employee numbers far outweigh the Federal Reserve and Treasury's employee numbers

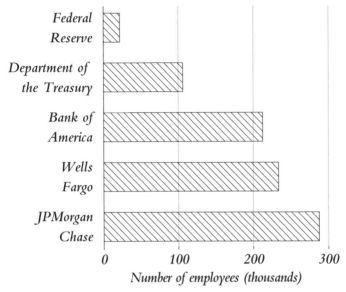

Number of employees (thousands)

Sources: Board of Governors of the Federal Reserve, Office of Personnel Management, Bank of America, and Statista.
Note: Federal Reserve employees include employees of the Board of Governors (3,000) and employees of the 12 regional Federal Reserve banks (19,288). Also note that of the 109,145 employees of the Department of the Treasury, 85 percent are solely in the Internal Revenue Service.

CBDC "would also require a central bank to take on new operational tasks such as credit risk and know your customer (KYC) analysis."[6] As noted in Chapter 2, the Reserve Bank of India issued a similar warning when it said that a CBDC would "put additional burden on the central banks in terms of managing customer on-boarding [as well as] KYC and AML checks[—]which may prove difficult and costly to the central bank."[7] Taken as a whole, compliance with the Bank Secrecy Act regime—what Greene and the Reserve Bank of

India referred to when citing "KYC and AML analysis"—cost U.S. financial institutions an estimated $45.9 billion in 2022.[8] That compliance involved identifying customers, monitoring transactions, employing software to flag activity trends, training employees, securing the confidentiality of files, and much more.

Compliance, however, is just one element to consider. There would also be the need to develop departments to handle the point-of-sale systems, the web interface, marketing, and customer support.[9] Were all of this not enough, then there are the layers of administrative staff—such as accounting, human resources, and facilities—that must be considered to keep this new mass expansion of employees in check and operating effectively. As Lawrence H. White, professor of economics at George Mason University, has warned in response to past central bank expansions, serving the public "requires more than merely setting up a website" and letting people set up accounts—and even that can be a challenge for governments.[10]

The last point to consider is that the government is ill-suited to offer retail services.[11] Between waiting on hold with the IRS for what might feel like an eternity to the seemingly never-ending lines at the Department of Motor Vehicles, people rarely enjoy interacting with the government.[12] This experience is so common that Presidents Joe Biden, Barack Obama, and Bill Clinton all issued executive orders calling for the federal government to offer a better "customer experience."[13] Yet not much has changed over these 30 years partly because government agencies do not have the same incentives to deliver services as private companies. Government policies often fail because they rely on top-down planning, become stagnant in the absence of market forces, and are often driven by bureaucratic inertia.[14] It is likely for these reasons that Barry Eichengreen, professor of economics and political science at the University of California, Berkeley, has said it is by "no means obvious" that "central banks can provide electronic payment services more efficiently than Visa or PayPal."[15] In fact, Lawrence White has argued, "Given the government's poor record on efficiency, the likely outcome would be a system that falls short on customer service or loses money at taxpayers' expense—or both."[16]

It is likely due to many of these concerns that the Federal Reserve proposed an intermediated CBDC model in which banks and other private financial institutions would take on some of the tasks considered here. In fact, many central banks around the world have sought out "public–private partnerships" to contract out the work on their CBDC development.[17] Still, offloading some of the work to the private sector is far from a panacea.

Nigeria's initial CBDC failures are a prime example of how offloading the work to a private company can cause even more problems for a central bank.[18] When the Central Bank of Nigeria publicly launched its CBDC (the eNaira), reports quickly emerged that the mobile app simply didn't work as advertised. The app received so many negative reviews that it was removed from the Google Play Store.[19] Despite the app later being reuploaded, the CBDC struggled to gain any adoption. The Central Bank of Nigeria later announced that it was looking for a new partner to redesign and improve its CBDC, but the reputational damage to the central bank had already been done.[20] Few people would likely recognize the name of the company behind the CBDC, but the central bank's failure was plastered across international headlines.

The Eastern Caribbean Central Bank faced a similar problem when its CBDC experienced technical failures.[21] And as described in Chapter 7, it was the Eastern Caribbean Central Bank that came under fire when the CBDC system went offline for months.

Cases like these may seem extreme, but they illustrate why contracting out work is not a panacea for a central bank facing the daunting task of transforming into a consumer-facing commercial bank. Even if the system runs relatively smoothly, things as mundane as long hold lines for customer service and glitches in the apps will suddenly become the fault of the central bank—regardless of whether those issues are contracted out.

Politicizing, and Undermining, the Federal Reserve

If shifting the focus from policy strategies to retail operations were not enough of a challenge in and of itself, there is also the risk that a CBDC would further politicize the Federal Reserve. Like many problems exacerbated by CBDCs, the politicization of the Federal Reserve and erosion of its independence has been a concern since long before the CBDC conversation began.[22] In fact, it had become such an issue that in 2019 four former chairs of the Federal Reserve—Paul Volcker, Alan Greenspan, Ben Bernanke, and Janet Yellen—cowrote an op-ed in the *Wall Street Journal* titled, "America Needs an Independent Fed."[23]

The independence of the Federal Reserve can be a difficult thing to assess though. At times, it seems the Federal Reserve has too much independence as these unelected officials attempting to steer the economy have little to no accountability.[24] Yet at other times, it seems the Federal Reserve has too little independence as politicians try to use it as a means for backdoor spending.[25] As James Dorn, senior fellow at the Cato Institute, has explained, "In conducting monetary policy, the [Federal Reserve] needs to be accountable to political institutions, yet independent of political pressures to finance budget deficits or use the printing press to satisfy special interests."[26] In considering this balance, the creation of a CBDC would risk an increased politicization of the Federal Reserve by turning it into an even more alluring target.

At a legislative markup where Congress was considering prohibiting the creation of a U.S. CBDC, Rep. Mike Flood (R-NE) called attention to the unique threat that a CBDC would pose to the Federal Reserve's independence, noting that a CBDC "could be used to prevent certain types of disfavored purchases, block certain disfavored people from using our financial system, or monitor the payment activities of political opponents." He added, "That is an enormous amount of power, and that power would put tremendous political pressure on the Federal Reserve."[27] He is right. With each expansion of the Federal Reserve, the central bank has become a bigger target for politicians.[28]

Although Representative Flood is a Republican, this risk is a danger to Republicans and Democrats alike. The danger simply depends on who is in control of leadership. When Democrats are in control, there could be pressure to use the Federal Reserve's new powers to go after gun shops. When Republicans are in control, the target could be labor unions.[29] In both cases, the Federal Reserve is caught in the middle. That is not a place any central bank should want to be in.

These political swings would risk jeopardizing the central bank's credibility. Just like in the event of a hack or a data breach, political pressures steering the Federal Reserve would rightly be viewed as vulnerabilities in the system that could undermine its overall performance.[30] The Federal Reserve already has enough on its plate in attempting to uphold its existing responsibilities to maintain stable prices, moderate long-term interest rates, and maximum employment. In fact, those limited responsibilities may already be beyond the Federal Reserve's reach.[31] However, as the four chairs of the Federal Reserve previously warned, "History, both here and abroad, has shown repeatedly . . . that an economy is strongest and functions best when the central bank acts independently of short-term political pressures and relies solely on sound economic principles and data."[32] Comparing measures of central bank independence against average inflation does seem to suggest that more independence leads to better results.[33]

Yet it's not just the Federal Reserve's direct performance in terms of fulfilling its mandate that would be jeopardized by these political swings. As Federal Reserve chair Jerome Powell has acknowledged, "The public's trust is really the [Federal Reserve's] and any central bank's most important asset."[34] Yet, political pressures on a CBDC could lead the public to question the Federal Reserve and even the dollar itself.[35] In fact, even the suspicion of political pressures may generate criticism as people try to understand how the Federal Reserve gained so many new powers through the launch of a CBDC and policy failures still occur. Again, that is not a position any central bank should want to be in.

In 2012, Charles Plosser, former president of the Federal Reserve Bank of Philadelphia, warned of the careful balance that must be struck to achieve central bank independence. He said, "It is simply good governance and wise economic policy to maintain a healthy separation between those responsible for tax and spending policy and those responsible for money creation."[36] And he went on to say that "it is equally important that independent central banks be constrained" from expanding into fiscal policy on their own accord.[37] Perhaps most notable, however, was Plosser's recommendation to maintain accountable independence: establish a narrow mandate for the central bank's goal, a restriction on what the central bank can do, and a rule for the central bank's policy decisions.[38] Introducing a CBDC would run counter to this recommendation.

Conclusion

Charles Calomiris, professor of finance at Columbia Business School, warned in a 2019 *Wall Street Journal* op-ed, "There are many levers that politicians can, and do, employ to influence monetary policy."[39] He added, "True independence comes from making it harder for politicians to pull those levers."[40] To introduce a CBDC would be to introduce a whole new set of levers with vast political capabilities. Politicians may try to justify the short-term gains, but the long-term costs to a central bank's performance and credibility are not worth it. Despite the excitement that the CBDC conversation has generated around central bankers and the vast powers a CBDC could introduce, it is not without costs. Central bankers should avoid the temptation to become so preoccupied with what they could do that they miss what they should do. If they fail to avoid this temptation, it could be the central bank itself that bears many of the costs.

9

FIGHTING BACK

The central focus of this book has been to first dispel the myths around the supposed benefits of CBDCs and then assess their risks. As we have seen thus far, a CBDC would spell doom for what little financial privacy remains. A CBDC would give the government an unprecedentedly powerful tool for financial control. A CBDC would destabilize the existing banking system and stamp out the rise of cryptocurrency. A CBDC would put the security of the economy as a whole at risk. And a CBDC would even jeopardize central banks themselves. But perhaps worst of all, a CBDC would offer little to no unique benefit to offset these risks. Choices are about tradeoffs. And when it comes to whether to adopt a CBDC, the choice is clear. The only "benefit" of CBDCs is for governments seeking to solidify their control over money and finance.

With that in mind, what can be done to fight back against the rise of CBDCs? Unfortunately, CBDCs are still very much an unknown issue. When the Cato Institute surveyed the American public on the topic in early 2023, 49 percent of respondents said that they didn't know enough to have an opinion about CBDCs.[1] That number closely mirrors what the CFA Institute found in a global survey in the summer of 2023.[2] So simply talking about CBDCs, sharing this book, and raising awareness about what a CBDC might mean for society are the first steps in turning the tide.

The story doesn't end there. Congress also has a role to play. Prohibiting the Federal Reserve and the Treasury Department from issuing a CBDC on their own accord will require legislation. (Examples of appropriate legislative language can be found in Appendix B.) As of this writing, many members of Congress have already introduced legislation. Although each bill differs on technical details, all of them seek to block the launch of a CBDC—in one form or another—in the United States.[3]

However, efforts to raise awareness and rein in the government should not stop with prohibiting the Federal Reserve and Treasury Department from issuing a CBDC. The primary focus of this book has been about CBDCs. However, you may have noticed a second story throughout these chapters—namely, that the existing financial system is hardly a bastion of freedom. In fact, across many areas, a CBDC would not create problems out of thin air. Instead, a CBDC would make existing problems worse.

It's time to repeal the laws and regulations that have restricted Americans' financial freedom, that have deputized banks as de facto law enforcement investigators, and that have blocked potentially new sources of competition. After more than 50 years of the ever-expanding Bank Secrecy Act regime, it's time to carve out a new path.[4] As Supreme Court justice Sonia Sotomayor noted, it's time to "reconsider the premise that an individual has no reasonable expectation of privacy" when sharing information with third parties, as this "approach is ill suited to the digital age."[5]

Furthermore, although a CBDC would not offer benefits like financial inclusion, faster payments, better monetary policy, and a stronger dollar, that doesn't mean those are not goals worth pursuing. For example, Congress can and should improve the strength of the dollar. But the focus should be on improving what has made the dollar strong already. That means Congress should work on creating stronger financial privacy protections, removing government roadblocks to faster payment speeds, and requiring better transparency in monetary governance.[6] All of these improvements would likely benefit the dollar's international status—and none of these changes would require reinventing the system from scratch.

After decoding what a CBDC might mean for the future of money, the future may seem grim. However, it doesn't have to be. The choice is ours to make. Rather than entrench years of policy mistakes and government failures in the launch of a CBDC, it's time to carve out a new path for the future of money.

Appendix A

Central bank digital currency (CBDC): a digital, national currency that is a liability of that nation's central bank.

Retail central bank digital currency (retail CBDC): a CBDC meant for retail, or consumer, use. Although the technical details differ significantly, it would generally resemble a prepaid card that is provided by the central bank.

Intermediated central bank digital currency (intermediated CBDC): a CBDC provided for retail use, but the accounts or wallets in which those CBDCs are held are maintained by private financial institutions (e.g., banks, credit unions, fintech firms).

Wholesale central bank digital currency (wholesale CBDC): a CBDC restricted to financial institutions for use during interbank settlement. In other words, a wholesale CBDC would serve as a way to send money between banks.

Synthetic central bank digital currency (synthetic CBDC): a CBDC in name only. The use of this term is not recommended because it is used to refer to a stablecoin with the reserves backing its value held in a central bank master account. Therefore, it is not a CBDC at all.

Account-based central bank digital currency: a CBDC where the central bank knows how many CBDCs are in circulation and where each unit of the CBDC is stored because ownership and use depend on individuals having a CBDC account.

Token-based central bank digital currency: a CBDC where the central bank knows how many CBDCs are in circulation, but not where they are stored.

Appendix B

This appendix offers sample legislative language to prevent the creation of a central bank digital currency (CBDC) and offer improvements to the existing system. This sample language is for educational purposes only.

Preventing the Creation of a CBDC

To prevent the risks to financial privacy, financial freedom, free markets, and cybersecurity that a CBDC would pose, Congress should explicitly prohibit both the Federal Reserve and the Department of the Treasury from issuing a CBDC in any form. To do so, Congress could amend the Federal Reserve Act as follows:[1]

1. Definitions—
   a. A central bank digital currency is defined as a digital liability of the U.S. government issued or minted by the Federal Reserve or the Department of the Treasury.

2. Section 13 of the Federal Reserve Act is amended
    by adding after the 14th undesignated paragraph
    (12 U.S.C. 347d) the following:

    a. The Board of Governors of the Federal Reserve
        System, Federal Reserve banks, or any desig-
        nated agents may not offer products or services
        directly to an individual, maintain an account
        on behalf of an individual, mint a central bank
        digital currency, issue a central bank digital cur-
        rency directly to an individual, or issue a central
        bank digital currency to an individual through
        an intermediary or other designated agent.

    b. No Federal Reserve bank may hold central
        bank digital currency minted or issued by the
        United States Government as assets or liabili-
        ties on their balance sheets or use digital cur-
        rencies minted or issued by the United States
        Government as part of fulfilling the require-
        ments under section 2A.

To prohibit the Treasury from issuing a CBDC, Congress
should limit the Treasury's authority to expand existing
offerings (e.g., TreasuryDirect). For example, the Treasury
has already expanded its authority to issue savings bonds to
design the myRA (my Retirement Account) program and
others have proposed further expanding TreasuryDirect to
become a sort of CBDC account.[2] Congress should amend
31 U.S.C. Section 3105 to prohibit the Treasury from offering or maintaining accounts on behalf of individuals. Likewise, Congress should more explicitly limit the capabilities
and payments through the Treasury's Direct Express cards
with respect to CBDCs.[3]

Finally, to prevent the Federal Reserve from acting on any legal ambiguities or gray areas, Congress should also include a "Sense of the Congress" resolution to put the full legislative intent on record.

1. Sense of the Congress
    a. It is the sense of the Congress that—
        i.   the Federal Reserve does not have the authority to launch a retail, intermediated, or wholesale central bank digital currency.
        ii. the Department of the Treasury does not have the authority to launch a retail, intermediated, or wholesale central bank digital currency.
        iii. a proposal for a central bank digital currency will not be considered for authorization unless it is open-source, permissionless, private, and unable to be altered after its launch.

Limiting Further Expansions of the Federal Reserve

The Federal Reserve's ability to ignore costs and crowd out the private sector came up during the initial announcement of FedNow. In 2019 congressional testimony, George Selgin, director emeritus of the Cato Institute's Center for Monetary and Financial Alternatives, warned that the Federal Reserve's status as a monetary monopoly and regulator gives it an unfair legal advantage over private payments systems.[4] He further warned that, although the Depository Institutions Deregulation and Monetary Control Act of 1980 is meant to limit the Federal Reserve's activity, the legislation is far from binding. The legislation requires neither a formal cost-recovery period nor a third-party audit. In other words, the Federal Reserve—unlike its private-sector counterparts—does not have to worry about recouping costs and can avoid doing so to undercut the market. Much as Selgin warned, the Federal Reserve revealed in late 2023 that it had spent $545 million to build FedNow and would continue to keep participation fees at $0.00 for another year to spur its adoption.[5]

To prevent the Federal Reserve from further encroaching on the private sector, Congress should amend the Depository Institutions Deregulation and Monetary Control Act of 1980 to strengthen the explicit requirement for the Federal Reserve to recover its costs when exploring new initiatives.[6] To do so, Congress should strike 12 U.S.C. Section 248a(c)(3) and replace it with the following language:

1. Over ~~the long run~~ **a period of no more than five years**, fees shall be established on the basis of all direct and indirect costs actually incurred in providing the Federal Reserve services priced, including interest on items credited prior to actual collection, overhead, and an allocation of imputed costs which takes into account the taxes that would have been paid and the return on capital that would have been provided had the services been furnished by a private business firm, except that the pricing principles shall give due regard to competitive factors and the provision of an adequate level of such services nationwide.

Finally, Congress should also require that the Federal Reserve's compliance with the Depository Institutions Deregulation and Monetary Control Act's cost-recovery provisions be subject to regular audits by third parties.[7]

Improving Financial Privacy

To establish stronger financial privacy protections, Congress should remove the exceptions in the Right to Financial Privacy Act. Doing so would merely require that law enforcement and other government agencies seek a warrant for Americans' financial records. To do so, Congress should strike 12 U.S.C. Section 3413(a)–(r) and 12 U.S.C. Section 3414(a)–(e). Removing these sections will not affect the exceptions provided for customer disclosures, subpoenas, or warrants in 12 U.S.C. Section 3402.

The Right to Financial Privacy Act should also be strengthened with respect to the formal written requests that it allows government authorities to issue when there is no warrant or subpoena authority available. Congress should strike 12 U.S.C. Section 3408(2), as regulations should not be considered an avenue for circumventing the Fourth Amendment protections this law sought to establish. Likewise, Congress should strike 12 U.S.C. Section 3408(4)(A)2, because Americans should not have to sue the government to have their rights respected when it has already been judged that the authority for a warrant or subpoena does not exist.

Congress should repeal the Bank Secrecy Act in its entirety. Short of that, it should, at the very least, repeal the sections of the Bank Secrecy Act that require financial institutions to report on their customers.[8] To do so, Congress should amend 12 U.S.C. Sections 3402, 3413, and 3414 as well as 31 U.S.C. Sections 5313–16, 5318(a)(2), 5318A, 5321, 5325, 5326, 5331–32, 5341–42, and 5351–55.

To the extent that reporting requirements may still exist after amending the Right to Financial Privacy Act and the Bank Secrecy Act, Congress should require annual inflation adjustments for all Bank Secrecy Act reporting thresholds. To do so, Congress could use the following language:[9]

1. Not later than the end of the 180-day period beginning on the date of the enactment of this Act, and annually thereafter, the Secretary of the Treasury shall revise regulations issued with respect to Section 5313 of Title 31, United States Code, to update each $10,000 threshold in such regulations to [insert inflation-adjusted amount as of the current day].

2. Section 5331 of Title 31, United States Code, is amended by striking "10,000" each place such term appears in heading or text and inserting "[insert inflation-adjusted amount as of the current day]."

3. Not later than the end of the 180-day period beginning on the date of the enactment of this Act, and annually thereafter, each Federal department or agency that issues regulations with respect to reports on suspicious transactions described under Section 5318(g) of Title 31, United States Code, shall update each $5,000 threshold amount in such regulations to [insert inflation-adjusted amount as of the current day] and each $2,000 threshold amount in such regulation to [insert inflation-adjusted amount as of the current day].

Likewise, if such reporting requirements are permitted to continue, Congress should require the Financial Crimes Enforcement Network (FinCEN) to publicly report the number of suspicious activity reports, or SARs, and currency transaction reports, or CTRs, that effectively curb financial crime. The report should detail how many reports are received, reviewed, and requested by other government agencies. In addition, FinCEN should report how many reports resulted in conviction, settlement, or additional charges in investigations unrelated to money laundering. The reports should make a clear distinction between criminal investigations that originated with SARs or CTRs and criminal investigations that merely used existing SARs or CTRs to strengthen existing cases. To do so, Congress could use the following language:[10]

1. Annual Report.—Not later than one year after the date of enactment of this Act, and annually thereafter, the Attorney General, in consultation with the Secretary of the Treasury, Federal law enforcement agencies, the Director of National Intelligence, Federal functional regulators, and the heads of other appropriate Federal agencies, shall publish a publicly available report that contains statistics, metrics, and other information on the use of data derived from financial institutions reporting under the Bank Secrecy Act, including the number of reports that—

    A. have been received by the Financial Crimes Enforcement Network;

    B. have been reviewed by the Financial Crimes Enforcement Network;

    C. have been requested by other government agencies;

    D. have led to a secondary investigation by the Financial Crimes Enforcement Network;

    E. have led to further procedures by law enforcement agencies, including the use of a subpoena, warrant, or other legal process;

    F.   have resulted in a conviction or settlement; and

    G.   have resulted in additional charges in investigations unrelated to money laundering.

Congress should also eliminate 26 U.S.C. Section 6050I because no American should be forced by law to report on the activity of another American—especially when that activity is only between two parties. Yet, 26 U.S.C. Section 6050I requires exactly that when Americans choose to use cash or cryptocurrencies.[11] This section should be repealed in its entirety. Between blockchain forensics and traditional investigations, plenty of tools are already available to law enforcement; Americans should not and need not be forced to become informants on one another against their will.[12]

Finally, Congress should turn its focus toward the future by enacting protections for two-party, or peer-to-peer, transactions. Holding cryptocurrency in a "self-hosted" wallet is merely the digital equivalent of holding physical cash in a traditional wallet. It gives wallet owners complete control over what's held inside it and, to the extent that they want to do so, the ability to maintain their privacy. Congress should not allow financial surveillance to be expanded to cover self-hosted wallets and peer-to-peer exchanges. To do so, Congress could use the following language:[13]

    1.   In General—No agency head may prohibit or otherwise restrict the ability of a covered user to—

        A.   use cryptocurrency or its equivalent for such user's own purposes, such as to purchase goods and services for the user's own use; or

        B.   conduct transactions through a self-hosted wallet.

Expanding Freedom for Currency Competition

To clarify the application of legal tender laws as far as a CBDC might be concerned, Congress could use the following language to amend 31 U.S.C. Section 5103:

1. United States coins and currency (~~including~~ **defined as** Federal reserve notes and circulating notes of Federal reserve banks and national banks) are legal tender for all debts, public charges, taxes, and dues. Foreign gold or silver coins are not legal tender for debts. **Legal tender status does not require private businesses, persons, or organizations to accept United States coins and currency as payments for goods and services.**

Congress should also amend 18 U.S.C. Section 486, in which the law specifically forbids not just counterfeit coins, but also coins of original design. To do so, Congress should strike "or of original design" 18 U.S.C. Section 486 and replace it with the following language:

1. Whoever, except as authorized by law, makes or utters or passes, or attempts to utter or pass, any coins of gold or silver or other metal, or alloys of metals, intended for use as current money, whether in the resemblance of coins of the United States or of foreign countries, ~~or of original design,~~ shall be fined under this title or imprisoned not more than five years, or both.

Capital gains taxes act as a deterrent to cryptocurrency use and should be removed, at the very least where cryptocurrencies are used for transactions, although ideally, Congress should amend the capital gains laws to level the competitive environment for other alternative currencies as well. First, capital gains tax rates are structured to incentivize long-term holding, which discourages what is generally considered "currency use." Second, the complexity of administering the tax creates an additional burden on would-be users of cryptocurrencies. Where a sales tax is usually a flat percentage added on to the bill, capital gains taxes require a cryptocurrency user to report the sales price, cost, timeline, and gain or loss for each transaction to the Internal Revenue Service. Specifically, users must record this information on Schedule D of Form 1040 to calculate the tax owed for each purchase of goods and services.[14]

The capital gains tax should be eliminated from transactions in which one uses cryptocurrencies to purchase goods and services. Although not ideal, the Virtual Currency Tax Fairness Act of 2022 would exempt personal transactions made in cryptocurrencies so long as the relevant gains are $200 or less.[15] However, there are three key changes that might improve the bill. The first would be to eliminate the $200 threshold while preserving the condition that a cryptocurrency is used for the purchase of goods and services (rather than to cash out). At a minimum, though, a second change would be to raise the threshold substantially ($10,000 or more) so that larger purchases could be made without additional taxation. Finally, a third change would be to scale the threshold for inflation.

Appendix C

THE RISE OF OPPOSITION TO CBDCs

To the extent this book is a reference for understanding the rise of central bank digital currencies (CBDCs), it might also be helpful to understand the rise of opposition to CBDCs. So to close out this book officially, the following quotes are from those who have spoken out against CBDCs. This list is not exhaustive, but it shows that policy analysts, academics, industry representatives, and even government officials themselves recognize that the risks of CBDCs far outweigh any purported benefits.[1]

> "CBDCs are especially dangerous as they could give the government complete control over all spending."
> —Kevin Dowd, Durham University[2]

> "You don't have to be a fan of the banking system status quo to see the surveillance danger in CBDC."
> —Lawrence H. White, George Mason University[3]

> "Technology and economic geopolitics can change rapidly, to be sure; but at least right now, the costs of introducing CBDC appear to outweigh the benefits."
> —Christina Parajon Skinner, Wharton School of the University of Pennsylvania[4]

"At some point, a CBDC that fails to provide a high degree of financial privacy will be used to monitor and censor the transactions of one's political enemies. It is foolish to think otherwise."
—William Luther, Florida Atlantic University[5]

"Central bank digital currencies are the bad idea that won't go away. There are simpler, more straightforward ways of solving the problems that CBDCs are deemed to address. Yet upwards of 130 countries worldwide are exploring the currencies. If you are in search of a bandwagon effect, this is it."
—Barry Eichengreen, University of California, Berkeley[6]

"What is ultimately at stake [with CBDCs] for western countries is not only the free-market economy but democracy itself."
—Patrick Schueffel, School of Management, Fribourg, Switzerland[7]

"CBDC is the latest attempt to expand their power at our expense by self-interested central bankers, which have done more in developed countries to expand their power at the expense of democracy over the past two decades than any other instrument of government."
—Charles Calomiris, Columbia Business School[8]

"By eliminating the private banking middleman, central bank digital currencies eliminate a key buffer that helps insulate individuals and firms from government prying and overreach."
—Richard Epstein and Max Raskin, New York University[9]

"I don't see any big failures in the market that require the public sector to step in and provide a digital euro."
—Ignazio Angeloni, European University Institute[10]

"The level of control that the government could exert over people would be limitless if money is purely electronic *and* provided solely and directly by the government. A CBDC would give federal officials complete control over the money going into—and coming out of—every person's account."
—Norbert Michel, Cato Institute[11]

"There's a tendency in politics to observe new innovation in markets and presume that, if it's important enough, government institutions must get in on the act. But the Treasury should think carefully about what a CBDC actually delivers that ongoing private sector innovation cannot. And [people] that care about economic and social liberties should be very wary of granting a free pass to the creation of new tools that could lead both to more government direction of investment and tighter paternalistic controls on private spending."
—Ryan Bourne, Cato Institute[12]

"America has plenty of digital currency. Every swipe you make, you're transacting in digital currency. Adding a new form of digital currency from the central bank does little to change the fundamental issues facing lower-income Americans."
—Aaron Klein, Brookings Institution[13]

"It isn't clear to me how you can have a retail CBDC and also have a functioning democracy in the long run."
—Chris Meserole, Brookings Institution[14]

"At best, a wholesale CBDC represents wasting taxpayer funds on a project that doesn't serve the Fed's stated mandate. At worst, it begins a slippery slope toward a retail CBDC and the associated economic and privacy risks."
—David Waugh, American Institute for Economic Research[15]

"In other words, those calling for the rollout of a CBDC are naïve to believe that this can be done without establishing a centralized surveillance system for all financial transacting. Quite simply, even if such surveillance is not included in the [initial] design, it would be trivial to add it at a later stage. Once a door to surveillance is opened, it is virtually impossible to close."
—Natalie Smolenski, Bitcoin Policy Institute[16]

"In a fully implemented CBDC system, governments could financially exclude individuals or entire groups of people with the press of a button, leaving them with nothing. Governments like the CCP [Chinese Communist Party] could target dissidents, sexual minorities, ethnic minorities, or religious minorities. If banknotes don't exist and access to government-issued digital cash is revoked, then they are truly helpless."
—Alex Gladstein, Human Rights Foundation[17]

"A CBDC creates a fully traceable and controllable digital currency that has vast implications for civil liberties and economic freedom. Rather than offering separation of money and state as found in Satoshi's innovation of Bitcoin, CBDCs completely merge the power of state and money in a way that will only prove harmful to individual liberty."
—Yaël Ossowski, Consumer Choice Center[18]

"CBDC projects around the world have painted a consistent picture of low uptake and poor outcomes, paired with real threats to human rights and civil liberties."
—Susannah Copson, Big Brother Watch[19]

"CBDCs represent a great irony, I think we can say. An essential goal of cryptocurrencies and their formation

was to escape central banks. Now the central banks themselves . . . have taken over this digital idea with the possible result of even great centralized monetary power than before."
—Alex J. Pollock, R Street Institute[20]

"More must be done overall to protect civil liberties and the stability of the American free market from the destructiveness of a CBDC. We need bipartisan efforts to protect financial privacy and oppose policies that go beyond the wishes of the governed."
—John Berlau and Ari Patinkin, Competitive Enterprise Institute[21]

"The United States dollar is [a] symbol of freedom and prosperity. A CBDC would present a threat to both symbols."
—Michael Faulkender and David Vasquez, America First Policy Institute[22]

"The issuance of a U.S. central bank digital currency is wholly unnecessary and would only further entrench the federal government's foothold in the U.S. banking and finance sector. It allows the federal government to better control and monitor payments—a direct assault on consumer privacy protections. A CBDC would also crowd out private digital assets and force technological innovation out of the U.S."
—Bryan Bashur, Americans for Tax Reform[23]

"A central bank digital currency is not simply paper currency in digital form: its adoption would have profound consequences for the U.S. financial system and economy."
—Gregory Baer, Bank Policy Institute[24]

"While there are no doubt opportunities for improvement, we believe most, if not all, [of these opportunities] can be addressed by innovations in the current financial services framework and through continued public-private partnerships, without the introduction of a novel digital currency that could destabilize the system."
—Madison Rose, Credit Union National Association[25]

"Contrary to popular belief, a U.S. CBDC is not necessary to 'digitize the dollar,' as the dollar is largely digital today. However, the issuance of a CBDC would fundamentally rewire our banking and financial system by changing the relationship between citizens and the Federal Reserve."
—Rob Morgan, American Bankers Association[26]

"[The] creation of a CBDC will introduce significant privacy and cybersecurity risks into the nation's monetary system and disrupt the stability of America's banking system."
—Deborah Matthews Phillips and Mickey Marshall, Independent Community Bankers of America[27]

"It's naive to think that a government that is currently combing through individual financial information will stop doing so when it has the formidable power of a CBDC."
—Sean Fieler, Equinox Partners[28]

"With a CBDC, central banks would have a backdoor directly into your bank account, as well as the means to monitor every digital transaction made."
—Dante Alighieri Disparte, Circle[29]

"CBDCs are a nightmare for civil liberties. They put governments at the center of every transaction, giving governments visibility into financial transactions and the ability to revoke money. This is the exact opposite of the purpose of cryptocurrency technology."
—Marta Belcher, Filecoin Foundation[30]

"CBDC systems, while nominally influenced by cryptocurrencies like bitcoin, are unlikely to be based on the distributed blockchain technology that keeps cryptocurrency base layers essentially hack-proof. That means the systems could become an unimaginably alluring target for hackers—with potential disruptions even bigger than the shutdown of a crucial gasoline pipeline."
—David Z. Morris, CoinDesk[31]

"A digital U.S. currency would be one of the most dangerous developments in history. When government can simply flip a switch to block all your transactions, it controls your entire life. We need a wall of separation between money and state."
—Justin Amash, former U.S. Representative (L-MI)[32]

"My principal concern with the domestic use case [of a CBDC] is the blurring of the line between monetary and fiscal policy."
—U.S. Rep. Jake Auchincloss (D-MA)[33]

"The prospect of government surveillance of Americans' individual financial transactions through a CBDC and Fed accounts raises serious privacy concerns, not to mention concerns about government control and politicization of loans, online payments, credit scores, tax compliance, federal contracts, monetary policy and the like."
—U.S. Rep. Andy Barr (R-KY)[34]

"I'm hard pressed to think how a private bank would have a specific incentive to take CBDC deposits. . . . I can't see [lending and deposits] existing in a CBDC system."
—U.S. Rep. Sean Casten (D-IL)[35]

"A CBDC would allow the government to spy on us. Congress needs to [stop] the Fed from developing a CBDC now!"
—U.S. Sen. Ted Cruz (R-TX)[36]

"A centrally managed, centrally controlled, Central Bank Digital Currency (CBDC) is a tool for coercion and control."
—U.S. Rep. Warren Davidson (R-OH)[37]

"Not only would this CBDC model centralize Americans' financial information, leaving it vulnerable to attack, but it could also be used as a surveillance tool that Americans should never tolerate from their own government."
—U.S. Rep. Tom Emmer (R-MN)[38]

"My concern is that once a CBDC is built, there will always be the potential for it to be abused."
—U.S. Rep. Mike Flood (R-NE)[39]

"[Let] me be unequivocally clear here for this audience: there is no support for a CBDC in Congress, except from those on the fringes who think somehow a CBDC might be an amazing solution to many unstated global problems."
—U.S. Rep. French Hill (R-AR)[40]

"There's no question about it; CBDCs are about containment, surveillance, and control."
—U.S. Rep. Mark Green (R-TN)[41]

"The United States doesn't need to create a Central
Bank Digital Currency to know it is a bad idea."
—U.S. Sen. Mike Lee (R–UT)[42]

"Republicans have consistently said the benefits of a
potential U.S. CBDC must outweigh the risks—these
reports fail to make the case. The Biden Administration
has not adequately identified what problems a CBDC
would solve or whether private sector payment solutions
could provide a better alternative."
—U.S. Rep. Patrick McHenry (R–NC)[43]

"The Biden administration's efforts to inject a
Centralized Bank Digital Currency is about surveillance
and control . . . a 'centralized digital dollar' which
will stifle innovation and promote government-sanc-
tioned surveillance. Florida will not side with economic
central planners; we will not adopt policies that threaten
personal economic freedom and security."
—Ron DeSantis, governor, Florida[44]

"We would not want a world in which the government
sees, in real time, every money transfer that anyone
makes with a CBDC."
—Jerome Powell, chair, Federal Reserve[45]

"As I have said before, the introduction of a U.S.
CBDC would come with a number of costs and risks,
including cyber risk and the threat of disintermediating
commercial banks, both of which could harm, rather
than help, the U.S. dollar's standing internationally."
—Christopher J. Waller, member, Federal Reserve
Board of Governors[46]

"I can see why China would do it. If they want to monitor every one of your transactions, you could do that with a central bank digital currency. You can't do that with Venmo. If you want to impose negative interest rates, you could do that with a central bank digital currency. You can't do that with Venmo. And if you want to directly tax customer accounts, you could do that with a central bank digital currency. You can't do that with Venmo. I get why China would be interested. Why would the American people be for that?"
—Neel Kashkari, president, Federal Reserve Bank of Minneapolis[47]

"In brief, the potential benefits of a Federal Reserve CBDC are unclear. Conversely, a Federal Reserve CBDC could pose significant and concrete risks."
—Randal Quarles, former vice chair, Federal Reserve[48]

"In addition, of course, we have Project CBDC [Central Bank Digital Currency], which, we think, has very little value added on the retail level."
—Felipe M. Medalla, governor, Central Bank of the Philippines[49]

"We haven't made a decision to issue [a CBDC] yet because we basically don't see a compelling need under current circumstances."
—Timothy Lane, deputy governor, Bank of Canada[50]

"To date, though, we have not seen a strong public policy case to move [toward a CBDC], especially given Australia's efficient, fast, and convenient electronic payments system."
—Philip Lowe, governor, Reserve Bank of Australia[51]

"Every time we tried to find a problem statement that a CBDC is trying to solve, it seems to be that [our] faster payments system upgrade is solving for it already."
—Sopnendu Mohanty, chief fintech officer, Monetary Authority of Singapore[52]

"CBDCs would give the government virtually complete control over the monetary system . . . but from an individual's perspective, a CBDC would be a historic blow to privacy and individual liberty."
—Joseph Wang, former Federal Reserve trader[53]

NOTES

Chapter 1

1. As of December 2023, nine countries and the eight islands making up the Eastern Caribbean Currency Union have launched CBDCs; 38 countries and Hong Kong have CBDC pilot programs; and 68 countries and two currency unions (the eurozone and the Economic and Monetary Community of Central Africa) are researching CBDCs as of this writing. For up-to-date assessments on CBDCs around the world, see Human Rights Foundation, "CBDC Tracker."

2. Howard Adler and Alex J. Pollock, "Why a Fed Digital Dollar Is a Bad Idea," RealClearMarkets, July 22, 2021.

3. Adler and Pollock, "Why a Fed Digital Dollar Is a Bad Idea."

4. Nicholas Anthony, "Decoding Biden's Executive Order on Cryptocurrency," *Cato at Liberty* (blog), Cato Institute, March 9, 2022; Nicholas Anthony, "CBDC Legislation Recap," *Cato at Liberty* (blog), Cato Institute, July 6, 2023; Nicholas Anthony, "Questions of CBDC Cronyism Emerge as Fed Launches Pilot," *Cato at Liberty* (blog), Cato Institute, December 1, 2022.

5. Emily Ekins and Jordan Gygi, "Poll: Only 16% of Americans Support the Government Issuing a Central Bank Digital Currency," Cato Institute, May 31, 2023.

Chapter 2

1. Norbert Michel, "CBDCs: Not Just a Different Form of Money," *Forbes*, March 6, 2023.

2. Michel, "CBDCs."

3. For additional details, see Nicholas Anthony, "Whose Liability Is It Anyway? CBDC Edition," *Cato at Liberty* (blog), Cato Institute, August 7, 2023.

4. The Federal Reserve advises people who want to replace damaged or contaminated bills to seek help from their local commercial bank. However, if the bills are mutilated, then people must contact the Department of the Treasury's Bureau of Engraving and Printing. Laura Taylor, "What to Do with Ripped, Torn or Damaged Money," *Open Vault* (blog), June 8, 2022.

5. Anthony, "Whose Liability Is It Anyway?"

6. In 2021, Americans made an average of 240 million debit transactions per day. "The Federal Reserve Payments Study: 2022 Triennial Initial Data Release," Board of Governors of the Federal Reserve System, 2022.

7. For a slightly deeper dive into the different CBDC models that explains the direct, indirect, synthetic, and wholesale models, see Appendix A and Nicholas Anthony and Norbert Michel, "A Breakdown of the Different CBDC Models," *Cato at Liberty* (blog), Cato Institute, February 10, 2023.

8. "Concept Note on Central Bank Digital Currency," Reports, Reserve Bank of India, October 7, 2022.

9. Emily Ekins, "79% Say It's 'Unreasonable' for Banks to Share What You Buy with the Government," *Cato at Liberty* (blog), Cato Institute, September 9, 2022; Nicholas Anthony, "The Right to Financial Privacy: Crafting a Better Framework for Financial Privacy in the Digital Age," Cato Institute Policy Analysis no. 945, May 2, 2023.

10. "Central Bank Digital Currency," Reserve Bank of India.

11. CNBC, "Fed Chair Powell Testifies before the House Committee on Monetary Policy," YouTube video, March 8, 2023.

12. Federal Reserve chair Jerome Powell is not the only central banker to recognize that wholesale CBDCs are not a major innovation. Fellow member of the Federal Reserve Board

Michelle Bowman and the then governor of the Reserve Bank of Australia Philip Lowe have said much the same. Moreover, a 2023 Bretton Woods Committee report said, "A wholesale CBDC alone is not much of an improvement over the existing regime in which central bank money is already moved digitally among banks and other financial intermediaries over payment rails operated by the central bank." Michelle W. Bowman, "Technology, Innovation, and Financial Services" (speech given at the VenCent Fintech Conference, Little Rock, AR, August 17, 2022); Philip Lowe, "Payments: The Future?" (speech given at the Australian Payments Network Summit, online, December 9, 2021); William C. Dudley, Anthony Elson, and Natalya Thakur, "Central Bank Digital Currencies: Design and Implementation in the Evolution of Sovereign Money," Bretton Woods Committee Brief no. 8, November 2023, p. 3.

13. Jon Durfee, Jesse Leigh Maniff, and Priyanka Slattery, "Examining CBDC and Wholesale Payments," FEDS Notes, September 8, 2023.

14. At worst, a wholesale CBDC may be better viewed as a pilot study for issuing a retail CBDC. For example, Indonesia's central bank has said it plans to issue a CBDC in three phases that begin with wholesale and end with retail. Bank Indonesia, "Project Garuda: Navigating the Architecture of Digital Rupiah."

15. Some have taken issue with the term "intermediated CBDC" because it could be confused with "financial intermediation." Where an "intermediated CBDC" refers to a CBDC model that puts banks or other private-sector actors in between individuals and the central bank, "financial intermediation" refers to the practice of a third party connecting an investor with a borrower. Common third parties include commercial banks, investment banks, mutual funds, and the like.

16. Board of Governors of the Federal Reserve System, "Money and Payments: The U.S. Dollar in the Age of Digital Transformation," Federal Reserve discussion paper, January 2022, p. 14.

17. Nicholas Anthony, "Introducing a CBDC Would Be a Catastrophe for the Banking System," *American Banker*, June 7, 2023; Anthony, "Whose Liability Is It Anyway?"

Chapter 3

1. Christopher J. Waller, "CBDC—A Solution in Search of a Problem?" (speech, American Enterprise Institute, Washington, August 5, 2021).

2. For examples of how CBDCs have captured public attention, see Nicholas Anthony, "Questions of CBDC Cronyism Emerge as Fed Launches Pilot," *Cato at Liberty* (blog), Cato Institute, December 1, 2022; Alexander William Salter, "Dangers of a Digital Dollar," *Wall Street Journal*, October 5, 2021; Randal Quarles, "Parachute Pants and Central Bank Money" (speech, 113th Annual Utah Bankers Association Convention, Sun Valley, ID, June 28, 2021); Andrew Ackerman, "Fed Prepares to Launch Review of Possible Central Bank Digital Currency," *Wall Street Journal*, October 4, 2021; Dion Rabouin, "The U.S. Is Losing the Global Race to Decide the Future of Money—And It Could Doom the Almighty Dollar," *Time*, September 21, 2021; John Kiff et al., "A Survey of Research on Retail Central Bank Digital Currency," International Monetary Fund Working Paper no. 2020/104, June 2020.

3. For example, the Treasury Department issued a report in 2022 that claimed a CBDC could lead to a payments system that is efficient, fosters innovation, facilitates cross-border transactions, and is environmentally sustainable. In addition, the Treasury claimed that a CBDC could promote financial inclusion, foster economic growth, protect against cyber risks, support individual rights, combat illicit activity, support sanctions, and preserve U.S. leadership. To say this list is overly optimistic is an understatement. U.S. Department of the Treasury, *The Future of Money and Payments: Report Pursuant to Section 4(b) of Executive Order 14067* (Washington: USDT, 2022).

4. Federal Deposit Insurance Corporation (FDIC), *FDIC National Survey of Unbanked and Underbanked Households* (Washington: FDIC, 2022).

5. Federal Deposit Insurance Corporation (FDIC), *FDIC National Survey*.

6. For example, see Christopher Condon, "Yellen Signals Interest in Backing Digital-Dollar Research," Bloomberg, February 22, 2021; Jared Wright, Henry Fingerhut, and Lauren Packard, "Central

Bank Digital Currencies Can Increase Financial Inclusion," Tony Blair Institute for Global Change, March 10, 2022; Bo Li, "Opening Remarks for Panel on the IMF Approach to Central Bank Digital Currency Capacity Development" (speech, International Monetary Fund 2023 Spring Meetings, Washington, April 12, 2023).

7. To be clear, the 72 percent referenced is a combination for the categories "Not at All Interested" and "Not Very Interested." Federal Deposit Insurance Corporation (FDIC), *FDIC National Survey*.

8. This analysis also applies to the fourth reason: bank account fees are too high.

9. Nicholas Anthony, "Only Six People Used the Postal Banking Pilot Program," *Cato at Liberty* (blog), Cato Institute, March 30, 2022.

10. For an extensive discussion of the Bank Secrecy Act—the law that started this surveillance regime—see Norbert Michel and Jennifer J. Schulp, "Revising the Bank Secrecy Act to Protect Privacy and Deter Criminals," Cato Institute Policy Analysis no. 932, July 26, 2022. For a brief breakdown, see Nicholas Anthony, "Why Don't Americans Have Stronger Financial Privacy Rights?," *Cato at Liberty* (blog), Cato Institute, October 28, 2021.

11. For reference, the "Patriot Act" is short for the "USA PATRIOT Act," or the "Uniting and Strengthening America by Providing Appropriate Tools Required to Intercept and Obstruct Terrorism Act of 2001."

12. Financial Crimes Enforcement Network, *Financial Crimes Enforcement Network (FinCEN) Year in Review for FY 2022* (Vienna, VA: FinCEN, 2022).

13. Banque de France, "Opportunities and Challenges of the Tokenisation of Finance," YouTube video, September 27, 2022.

14. "Public Trust in Government: 1958–2022," Pew Research, June 6, 2022.

15. Emily Ekins and Jordan Gygi, "Poll: Only 16% of Americans Support the Government Issuing a Central Bank Digital Currency," Cato Institute, May 31, 2023.

16. Dustin Volz and Byron Tau, "Little-Known Surveillance Program Captures Money Transfers between U.S. and More Than 20 Countries," *Wall Street Journal*, January 18, 2023.

17. In fact, Federal Reserve vice chair Lael Brainard's chief argument for the U.S. government to move forward with a CBDC is that it could take a long time to develop, and the United States might want one in the future. House Committee on Financial Services, "Digital Assets and the Future of Finance: Examining the Benefits and Risks of a U.S. Central Bank Digital Currency, (EventID=114689)," YouTube video, May 26, 2022.

18. Jonathan Cheng, "China Rolls Out Pilot Test of Digital Currency," *Wall Street Journal*, April 20, 2020.

19. The latest reports suggest that 120 million CBDC wallets have been opened. That suggests as much as 8.49 percent of China's population has opened a wallet, assuming no one has more than one wallet. However, this number may also be an overestimation because many accounts were opened to receive prizes from the Chinese government's lottery system and then never used again. Former People's Bank of China research director Zie Ping reported in 2022 that usage had been both low and highly inactive. Rae Wee, "China's Digital Yuan Transactions Seeing Strong Momentum, Says Cbank Gov Yi," Reuters, July 19, 2023; Jesse Coghlan, "Former Chinese Central Banker Says Digital Yuan 'Usage Has Been Low,'" Cointelegraph, December 30, 2022.

20. The terms "unbanked" and "underbanked" have a negative connotation and suggest someone is missing something. Yet, it's likely that some Americans simply prefer to be outside of the system, much like people living off the grid. To that end, it may be more accurate to consider not the number of people who are unbanked, but the number of people who are unbanked and want a bank account. Existing FDIC data suggest this subcategory makes up only 20.0 percent of the unbanked, or 0.9 percent of total U.S. households.

21. Given the history of financial surveillance in the United States, this condition would be a tough sell. Nicholas Anthony, "The Right to Financial Privacy: Crafting a Better Framework for Financial Privacy in the Digital Age," Cato Institute Policy Analysis no. 945, May 2, 2023.

22. George Selgin and Aaron Klein, "We Shouldn't Have to Wait for FedNow to Have Faster Payments," *American Banker*, February 28, 2020; "Flavors of Fast 2020: Real-Time Payments in the Americas," FIS, June 28, 2021.

23. Jim Himes, "Winning the Future of Money: A Proposal for a U.S. Central Bank Digital Currency," white paper, June 22, 2022; Vicki Hyman, "Your Guide to Understanding CBDCs," Mastercard Newsroom, August 1, 2023; John Kiff et al., "Research on Retail Central Bank Digital Currency."

24. Douglas J. Elliott and Larissa de Lima, "Central Bank Digital Currencies: Six Policy Mistakes to Avoid," Oliver Wyman, June 2021.

25. George Selgin, director, Cato Institute Center for Monetary and Financial Alternatives, "Facilitating Faster Payments in the U.S.," Testimony before the Senate Committee on Banking, Housing, and Urban Affairs, 116th Cong. 1st sess., September 25, 2019.

26. "Frequently Asked Questions," RTP, Clearing House.

27. Norbert Michel, "The Federal Reserve Should Not Compete with Private Firms," *Forbes*, December 16, 2018; "About RTP," RTP, Clearing House.

28. Greg Baer, "American Banker's Criticism of RTP: It's Like Rain on Your Wedding Day," Bank Policy Institute, July 30, 2019.

29. Selgin, "Facilitating Faster Payments in the U.S."; George Selgin, "Re: Potential Federal Reserve Actions to Support Interbank Settlement of Faster Payments: Docket No. OP-1625," Cato Institute, December 14, 2018.

30. *Hearing on Digital Dollar Dilemma: The Implications of a Central Bank Digital Currency and Private Sector Alternatives, Before the Committee on Financial Services, Subcommittee on Digital Assets, Financial Technology, and Inclusion,* 118th Cong. 1st sess. (September 14, 2023); *Hearing on Promises and Perils of Central Bank Digital Currencies, Before the Committee on Financial Services,* Subcommittee on National Security, Illicit Finance, and International Financial Institutions, 117th Cong. 1st sess. (July 27, 2021).

31. Selgin, "Facilitating Faster Payments in the U.S."; Selgin and Klein, "We Shouldn't Have to Wait for FedNow."

32. House Committee on Financial Services, "The Federal Reserve's Semi-Annual Monetary Policy Report (EventID =115416)," YouTube video, March 8, 2023; Nicholas Anthony, "Why Is the Fed Keeping Banker's Hours?," *Cato at Liberty* (blog), Cato Institute, April 10, 2023.

33. Philip Lowe, "Payments: The Future?" (speech, Australian Payments Network Summit, online, December 9, 2021).

34. "New Economy Forum: IMF Approach to Central Bank Digital Currency Capacity Development," International Monetary Fund, April 12, 2023.

35. Michelle W. Bowman, "Technology, Innovation, and Financial Services" (speech, VenCent Fintech Conference, Little Rock, AR, August 17, 2022).

36. Kiff et al., "Research on Retail Central Bank Digital Currency"; Mohammad Davoodalhosseini, Francisco Rivadeneyra, and Yu Zhu, "CBDC and Monetary Policy," Bank of Canada Staff Analytical Note no. 2020-4, February 2020; Francesca Carapella and Jean Flemming, "Central Bank Digital Currency: A Literature Review," FEDS Notes, November 9, 2020.

37. Thomas Franck, "Here's How the Fed Sets Interest Rates and How That Rate Has Changed over the Last Four Decades," CNBC, July 31, 2019; Sarah Foster, "What Is the Federal Funds Rate? How the Fed Sets Interest Rates, Explained," Bankrate, April 27, 2022; Ara Oghoorian, "How the Fed Sets Interest Rates," FPA.

38. George Selgin, William D. Lastrapes, and Lawrence H. White, "Has the Fed Been a Failure?," *Journal of Macroeconomics* 34, no. 3 (2012): 569–96.

39. Nicholas Anthony, "What Does Financial Privacy Mean for Liberty?," *Cato at Liberty* (blog), Cato Institute, July 10, 2023.

40. For more on the idea of cryptocurrency offering an escape hatch, see Jill Carlson, "Tunnels, Bunkers, and Escape Hatches: Defending Economic Rights under Fire," *Cato Journal* 41, no. 2 (2021): 259–69.

41. U.S. Department of the Treasury, *The Future of Money and Payments: Report Pursuant to Section 4(b) of Executive Order 14067* (Washington, USDT, 2022).

42. Christopher J. Waller, "The U.S. Dollar and Central Bank Digital Currencies" (speech, Digital Currencies and National Security Tradeoffs Symposium, Cambridge, MA, October 14, 2022).

43. Reps. French Hill (R-AR) and Bill Foster (D-IL), Letter to Jerome Powell, chair of the Board of Governors of the Federal Reserve System, September 30, 2019; Tatiana Koffman, "U.S. Moves Closer to Digital Dollar," *Forbes*, July 1, 2020; Andrew

Ackerman, "U.S. Lawmakers Look to Digital Dollar to Compete with China," *Wall Street Journal*, August 8, 2022; PM News, "European Central Bank (ECB) President Christine Lagarde Recently Fell Victim to a Prank," YouTube video, May 17, 2023.

44. China technically considers its CBDC to be a pilot program, but that terminology is misleading. In contrast to a closed, experimental trial that one might think of when hearing the term "pilot," China's CBDC currently has public users. Therefore, given that the CBDC is being used by real people to make real transactions, it is very much in its postlaunch phase. For additional details, see "CBDC Tracker," Human Rights Foundation.

45. As James Dorn notes, "The dollar has earned its status as a safe-haven currency because it is backed by trust in U.S. institutions that safeguard basic freedoms and private property rights. China lacks those institutions and trust." James A. Dorn, "China's Digital Yuan: A Threat to Freedom," *Cato at Liberty* (blog), Cato Institute, August 25, 2021; Dean Cheng, Norbert J. Michel, and Klon Kitchen, "China's Cryptocurrency Plans Are about Power, Not Innovation," Heritage Foundation Issue Brief no. 5014, November 22, 2019.

46. "CBDC Tracker," Human Rights Foundation.

47. "The Current Situation in Nigeria: A USIP Fact Sheet," U.S. Institute of Peace, August 11, 2021; "Inflation, Consumer Prices (Annual %)—Nigeria," World Bank, accessed September 2023.

48. Nicholas Anthony, "Nigerians' Rejection of Their CBDC Is a Cautionary Tale for Other Countries," Cato Institute, March 6, 2023; Nicholas Anthony, "Nigeria's CBDC Was Not Chosen. It Was Forced," *Cato at Liberty* (blog), Cato Institute, May 15, 2023.

49. Just before the Nigerian government created a cash shortage, Central Bank of Nigeria Deputy Governor Kingsley Obiora said that all the eNaira needs to gain adoption is "a little push from the government." Anthony Osae-Brown, Mureji Fatunde, and Ruth Olurounbi, "Digital-Currency Plan Falters as Nigerians Defiant on Crypto," Bloomberg, October 25, 2022; Anthony, "Nigerians' Rejection of Their CBDC Is a Cautionary Tale"; Anthony, "Nigeria's CBDC Was Not Chosen."

50. "GDP (Current US$)—Bahamas, The," World Bank, accessed September 2023; "GDP (Current US$)," World Bank, accessed September 2023.

Chapter 4

1. Hester M. Peirce, "Statement of Hester M. Peirce in Response to Release No. 34-88890; File No. S7-13-19," U.S. Securities and Exchange Commission, May 15, 2020.

2. Nicholas Anthony, "Why Don't Americans Have Stronger Financial Privacy Rights?," *Cato at Liberty* (blog), Cato Institute, October 28, 2021.

3. Nicholas Anthony, "The Right to Financial Privacy: Crafting a Better Framework for Financial Privacy in the Digital Age," Cato Institute Policy Analysis no. 945, May 2, 2023.

4. For example, Lewis McLellan, editor of the Digital Monetary Institute at the Official Monetary and Financial Institutions Forum, has argued, "CBDCs are not a serious threat to the privacy of digital payments because we have so little to begin with." Lewis McLellan, "CBDCs Can Help Protect against Surveillance Capitalism," OMFIF, June 5, 2023. Elsewhere, John Paul Koning, a financial writer and blogger, has argued that the Canadian government already has significant controls over the financial system. John Paul Koning (@jp_koning), "'But JP, with a CBDC we'd be giving the government full control over our money.' Meanwhile, Canada's Department of Finance explains how it surgically froze 280 bank accounts, no CBDC necessary," X, November 24, 2022, 6:32 a.m.

5. *United States v. Miller*, 425 U.S. 435 (1976).

6. Norbert Michel and Jennifer J. Schulp, "Revising the Bank Secrecy Act to Protect Privacy and Deter Criminals," Cato Institute Policy Analysis no. 932, July 26, 2022.

7. Anthony, "The Right to Financial Privacy."

8. Anthony, "The Right to Financial Privacy"; Michel and Schulp, "Revising the Bank Secrecy Act."

9. For the relevant portions of the Patriot Act, see sections 311, 314, 326, 352, 356, and 359. Committees on Judiciary, Intelligence, Financial Services, International Relations, Energy and Commerce, Education and the Workforce, Transportation and Infrastructure, and Armed Services, Uniting and Strengthening America by Providing Appropriate Tools Required to Intercept and Obstruct Terrorism (USA Patriot) Act of 2001, U.S. House,

107th Cong., 1st Sess., Report no. 1073162, 2001; Bank Secrecy Act, 31 U.S.C. § 5318(g) and § 5318(g)(2)(A)(i)–(ii).

10. The law also established a formalized anti–money laundering program requirement whereby financial institutions are required to develop internal policies, employ a compliance officer, train employees, and conduct audits to guard against money laundering and terrorist financing. See 31 U.S.C. § 5318(h).

11. Anthony, "The Right to Financial Privacy."

12. U.S. Department of the Treasury, "Fact Sheet: Tax Compliance Proposals Will Improve Tax Fairness While Protecting Taxpayer Privacy," Featured Stories, October 19, 2021.

13. Michelle Hackman and Dustin Volz, "Secret Surveillance Program Collects Americans' Money-Transfer Data, Senator Says," *Wall Street Journal*, March 8, 2022.

14. Matthew Guariglia, "Here's How ICE Illegally Obtained Bulk Financial Records from Western Union," Electric Frontier Foundation, March 10, 2022.

15. For example, at the time, one could purchase two brand-new Corvettes for $10,000. Scott Kolecki, "1970 C3 Chevrolet Corvette Model Guide," CorvSport.

16. Michel and Schulp, "Revising the Bank Secrecy Act."

17. As noted by Patrick Schueffel, adjunct professor at the School of Management in Fribourg, Switzerland: "Undoubtedly some of these actions can also be taken under the current monetary regime. But CBDCs will facilitate matters: going forward these measures can be implemented on a keystroke, in real-time and centrally. No more lengthy data gathering, and alignment of parties will be required." Patrick Schueffel, "CBDCs: Pros and Cons—A Comprehensive List and Discussion of the Advantages and Disadvantages of Central Bank Digital Currency," *Journal of Digital Assets* 1, no. 2 (2023): 51.

18. "Financial Privacy in a Digital Era," Live Online Policy Forum, Cato Institute, April 21, 2022; Dante Alighieri Disparte, "Is America Losing the Digital-Currency Race?," Project Syndicate, July 2, 2021.

19. Jerome Powell, chair of the Board of Governors of the Federal Reserve System, Letter to Representative French Hill, November 19, 2019.

20. Hackman and Volz, "Secret Surveillance Program Collects Americans' Money-Transfer Data"; Financial Crimes Enforcement Network, Treasury Department, *Financial Crimes Enforcement Network (FinCEN) Year in Review for FY 2022* (Vienna, VA: FinCEN, 2022); Nicholas Anthony, "Reporting FinCEN's Suspicious Activity," *Cato at Liberty* (blog), Cato Institute, April 13, 2022.

21. Michel and Schulp, "Revising the Bank Secrecy Act"; Anthony, "The Right to Financial Privacy."

22. *United States v. Jones*, 565 U.S. 400 (2012).

23. Anthony, "The Right to Financial Privacy."

24. Anthony, "The Right to Financial Privacy."

25. Anthony, "The Right to Financial Privacy."

26. The third-party doctrine holds that Fourth Amendment protections do not apply when someone shares information with a third party like a bank, internet provider, or similar business. The doctrine emerged from a 1976 Supreme Court case, *United States v. Miller*, in which the Court held that one cannot reasonably expect privacy when providing information to a third party. In the case of bank account information, the Court wrote, "The depositor takes the risk, in revealing his [or her] affairs to another, that the information will be conveyed by that person to the Government." This ruling is what came to be known as the "third-party doctrine." The third-party doctrine was later reaffirmed in 1979 in *Smith v. Maryland*. *United States v. Miller*, 425 U.S. 435 (1976); *Smith v. Maryland*, 422 U.S. 735 (1979); Anthony, "Why Don't Americans Have Stronger Financial Privacy Rights?"

27. See 27:14, *Frontline*, PBS, "United States of Secrets, Part One (full documentary)," PBS, YouTube video, September 9, 2021; Jane Mayer, "The Secret Sharer," *New Yorker*, May 23, 2011.

28. See 27:14, *Frontline*, "United States of Secrets."

29. To their credit, the team retired because of their concerns about the misuse of their program. Bill Binney, one of the designers of ThinThread, said, "I should apologize to the American people. It's violated everyone's rights. It can be used to eavesdrop on the whole world." Mayer, "The Secret Sharer." See also 29:38, *Frontline*, "United States of Secrets."

30. *Bitcoin Magazine*, "Strategic Competition & Digital Currencies," YouTube video, September 27, 2023.

31. MacKenzie Sigalos, "Vitalik Buterin, the Man behind Ethereum, Talks Crypto and the U.S. Crackdown," CNBC, September 22, 2023.

32. Sigalos, "Vitalik Buterin Talks Crypto."

33. Sigalos, "Vitalik Buterin Talks Crypto."

34. See 1:36:58 and 1:37:37, Banque de France, "Opportunities and Challenges of the Tokenisation of Finance," streamed live on September 27, 2022, YouTube video; International Monetary Fund, "Cross-Border Payments—A Vision for the Future," IMF Seminar, October 19, 2020; Chris Giles, "BoE Governor Says 'Regulated' Central Bank Digital Currency Preferred Option," *Financial Times*, November 23, 2021.

35. Nicholas Anthony, "Questions of CBDC Cronyism Emerge as Fed Launches Pilot," *Cato at Liberty* (blog), Cato Institute, December 1, 2022.

36. William J. Luther, "Will a Digital Dollar Offer Financial Privacy?," American Institute for Economic Research, October 7, 2022.

37. Deborah Matthews Phillips and Mickey Marshall, Independent Community Bankers of America, Letter to Ann E. Misback, secretary of the Board of Governors of the Federal Reserve System, Request for Comment Regarding the Board of Governors of the Federal Reserve System Public Consultation Paper, *Money and Payments: The U.S. Dollar in the Age of Digital Transformation*, May 20, 2022.

38. Sam Sutton, "Banks, Crypto Lobby Clash with Lawmakers over Fed Digital Dollar," *Politico*, August 22, 2022.

39. Michel and Schulp, "Revising the Bank Secrecy Act"; Anthony, "The Right to Financial Privacy."

Chapter 5

1. International Monetary Fund, "Cross-Border Payments—A Vision for the Future," IMF Seminar, October 19, 2020.

2. Nicholas Anthony, "What Does Financial Privacy Mean for Liberty?," *Cato at Liberty* (blog), Cato Institute, July 10, 2023.

3. For example, anti-counterfeiting measures must be able to be embedded within the note itself. Therefore, the features are largely limited to a special paper blend, watermarks, color-shifting ink, a security thread, a security ribbon, serial numbers, and other features. As extensive as these features are, they are wholly different from the near-endless possibilities that could be coded within a digital dollar.

4. Sam Benstead, "Freedom or Slavery: the 'Britcoin' Conundrum," *Daily Telegraph*, August 14, 2021.

5. In Russia, the chair of the Duma Committee on the Financial Market, Anatoly Aksakov, said: "No matter how great the student's desire to use his mother's digital ruble for unhealthy sweets, it will not be possible to use the money for other purposes. The intended purpose of the money allocated by the parents to the child will be specified in a special smart contract. A similar approach is applicable when directing government funds to implement various programs by contractors or individuals. This budget money will be used in a targeted manner for the implementation of exactly those projects for which they were intended, which will lead to an increase in the efficiency of circulation of public funds." Elsewhere, one company hired by the Bank of England to develop a CBDC told Bloomberg, "Its technology would allow verification of a person's citizenship and for purchasing age-restricted products such as alcohol and cigarettes." Valery Filonenko, "Anatoly Aksakov: Children Will Not Be Able to Spend Digital Rubles on Just Anything," Publication of the Federal Assembly of the Russian Federation, July 12, 2023; Tom Rees, "Digital Pound May Verify Age for Alcohol and UK Citizenship," Bloomberg, July 7, 2023.

6. Arthur Pigou, *The Economics of Welfare* (London: Palgrave Macmillan, 1920).

7. Jeffrey Miron and Nicholas Anthony, "Cannabis Banking: A Clash between Federal and State Laws," *Cato at Liberty* (blog), Cato Institute, May 27, 2022.

8. Nicholas Anthony, "Unlock the Cannabis Industry for Financial Institutions," *Reason*, April 19, 2023.

9. In addition to undermining the growth of an entire industry, the federal government's refusal to reform cannabis policy also undermines the authority of state governments and the choices of state voters. It undermines the fundamental idea that the states are meant to serve as laboratories of democracy. So long as federal agents could come at any given moment to make an arrest, any state experiment would be weighed down from its full potential. The challenges that cannabis-related companies face in acquiring basic banking services is a clear example of how the deck can be stacked against states—and voters—seeking change that runs counter to federal policy. Yet looking beyond cannabis, this problem would only be exacerbated if the federal government becomes involved with every transaction via a CBDC.

10. Dominic Casciani, "Coronavirus: What Powers Do Police Have if People Break Covid Rules?," BBC News, January 12, 2021; Chloe Taylor, "Austrian Police Conduct Random Checks to Enforce Covid Lockdowns for the Unvaccinated," CNBC, November 17, 2021; Scott Neuman, "Australian Troops Will Help Enforce a Coronavirus Lockdown in Sydney," NPR, July 30, 2021; Lea Hunter, Betsy Pearl, and Kenny Lo, "Tracking Enforcement Measures for Violation of Stay-at-Home Orders," Center for American Progress, April 2, 2020.

11. Casciani, "What Powers Do Police Have if People Break Covid Rules?"

12. Charlie Wood, "Spain's Police Are Flying Drones with Speakers around Public Places to Warn Citizens on Coronavirus Lockdown to Get Inside," Business Insider, March 16, 2020.

13. Neuman, "Australian Troops Will Help Enforce Coronavirus Lockdown."

14. In August 2023, the Pheu Thai Party in Thailand announced it would give out 10,000 baht ($283) in digital money to all citizens upon its gaining control of the government with the condition that the money be spent within four kilometers (2.5 miles) of the recipients' homes and within six months. Nareerat Wiriyapong, "Pheu Thai's Digital Wallet Wins Support," Bangkok Post, August 25, 2023.

15. John Kiff et al., "A Survey of Research on Retail Central Bank Digital Currency," International Monetary Fund Working Paper no. 2020/104, June 26, 2020; National Community Reinvestment Coalition, "Discerning a Regulatory Approach Crypto Currencies and Digital Assets," Just Economy Conference, Washington, YouTube video, June 16, 2022; Wolfram Seidemann, "CBDC Systems Should Focus on Programmable Payments," Official Monetary and Financial Institutions Forum, July 27, 2021; "How to Bring the Benefits of Programmability to CBDC," Giesecke+Devrient, December 8, 2021; Wiriyapong, "Pheu Thai's Digital Wallet Wins Support."

16. Nick Anthony (@EconWithNick), "And here we have Deputy Managing Director of the IMF sharing how central bank digital currency (CBDC) would allow the government to precisely control what people can and cannot spend their money on," X, October 15, 2022, 1:12 p.m.

17. "Supplemental Nutrition Assistance Program (SNAP)," District of Columbia Department of Human Services, accessed September 20, 2023.

18. Mohammad Davoodalhosseini, Francisco Rivadeneyra, and Yu Zhu, "CBDC and Monetary Policy," Bank of Canada Staff Analytical Note no. 2020-4, February 2020; Ulrich Bindseil, "Tiered CBDC and the Financial System," European Central Bank Working Paper no. 2351, January 2020; James Mackintosh, "Digital Currencies Pave Way for Deeply Negative Interest Rates," *Wall Street Journal*, September 8, 2021; "A Shift from Paper to Virtual Cash Will Empower Central Banks," *The Economist*, July 23, 2020.

19. Andy Haldane, "The Real Scandal of Central Bank Digital Currency," *Financial Times*, July 31, 2023. Although a CBDC makes positive and negative interest rates much more feasible, that's not to say they are completely impossible with cash. John Paul Koning, "Paying Interest on Cash," *Moneyness* (blog), January 25, 2018.

20. Emily Parker, "'Basically a Savior': Why Crypto Is So Popular in Turkey," CoinDesk, October 25, 2022; Medha Singh and Lisa Pauline Mattackal, "Cryptoverse: Digital Coins Lure Inflation-Weary Argentines and Turks," Reuters, May 2, 2023.

21. George Selgin, director emeritus of the Cato Institute's Center for Monetary and Financial Alternatives, has documented how the changing demand for money can be observed in Canada between 1880 and 1909 when migrant farmers would "cash out" at the end of each growing season—showcasing a seasonal demand for money. However, Selgin's work goes far beyond just the seasonal demand for money. His work also explores how the government restricted what is commonly, but inaccurately, referred to as a free banking era in U.S. history and how those restrictions undermined banks in the United States relative to their Canadian counterparts. George Selgin, "New York's Bank: The National Monetary Commission and the Founding of the Fed," Cato Institute Policy Analysis no. 793, June 21, 2016.

22. Implementing negative rates could also raise questions regarding the Fifth Amendment's protection against the government taking a person's property without compensation.

23. For a full discussion of this problem, see Chapter 6.

24. Andrey Sergeenkov, "China Crypto Bans: A Complete History," CoinDesk, September 29, 2021; Nicholas Anthony, "India Seeks to Criminalize Cryptocurrencies," Foundation for Economic Education, March, 26, 2021; Sebastian Sinclair, "Nigeria's Central Bank: We Didn't Ban Crypto Trading," CoinDesk, March 22, 2021.

25. Davoodalhosseini, Rivadeneyra, and Zhu, "CBDC and Monetary Policy"; Eswar S. Prasad, "The Case for Central Bank Digital Currencies," *Cato Journal* 41, no. 2 (2021): 251–58.

26. "Jimmy Lai—Recipient of the 2023 Milton Friedman Prize for Advancing Liberty," Cato Institute video, 10:05, May 19, 2023; Elaine Yu, "Hong Kong Police Arrest Apple Daily Editor under China National Security Law," *Wall Street Journal*, June 18, 2021.

27. Tony Munroe, "HK's Apple Daily Raided by 500 Officers over National Security Law," Reuters, June 17, 2021.

28. Andrew Osborn, "Russia Freezes Bank Accounts Linked to Opposition Politician Navalny," Reuters, August 8, 2019.

29. Nicholas Anthony, "How Canada Made the Case for Cryptocurrency, Not CBDCs," *Cato at Liberty* (blog), Cato Institute,

March 2, 2022; "Trudeau Invokes Emergencies Act for First Time Ever in Response to Protests," CBC News, February 14, 2022, YouTube video.

30. Mike McIntire and Michael H. Keller, "Canadians Are Responsible for Roughly Half of the Money Raised Online for the Trucker Convoy, Leaked Data Shows," *New York Times*, February 14, 2022.

31. Nicholas Anthony, "The Right to Financial Privacy: Crafting a Better Framework for Financial Privacy in the Digital Age," Cato Institute Policy Analysis no. 945, May 2, 2023.

32. Alan Zibel and Brent Kendall, "Probe Turns Up Heat on Banks," *Wall Street Journal*, August 7, 2013.

33. Howard Anglin, "In Our Cashless Society, We Need to Take Digital Jail Seriously," The Hub (Canada), February 22, 2022.

34. Civil forfeiture goes beyond seizing money alone. Government authorities have also used the policy to seize other property. For example, there have been cases of authorities seizing jewelry, books, and vehicles. "Civil Forfeiture," Institute for Justice; "Asset Forfeiture Abuse," American Civil Liberties Union; "Why Civil Asset Forfeiture Is Legalized Theft," Leadership Conference on Civil and Human Rights, July 23, 2015; "US Private Vaults Seizure," Institute for Justice; "Eagle Pass Forfeiture," Institute for Justice.

35. Civil asset forfeiture is another topic that could be a book of its own. For more information, see the ongoing work by the Institute for Justice and American Civil Liberties Union. "Civil Forfeiture," Institute for Justice; "Asset Forfeiture Abuse," American Civil Liberties Union.

36. "Civil Forfeiture," Institute for Justice.

37. Michael Sallah et al., "Stop and Seize," *Washington Post*, September 6, 2014; *United States of America v. Brian Moore, Jr.*, Civil Case no. 1:21-cv-03847-TWT (11th Cir. 2023); *Martin v. Federal Bureau of Investigation, et al.*, Civil Case no. 1:23-cv-00618 (D.C. Distr. Ct. 2023); *United States of America v. Starling*, Case No. 22-659 (2nd Cir. 2023); *Empyreal Enterprises, LLC, d/b/a Empyreal Logistics v. USA, et al.*, Case 5:22-cv-00094-JWH-SHK (C.D. Cal. 2022); *Lara v. State of Nevada, et al.*, Case No. CV21-01595

(2nd J.D.C Nev. 2021); *United States of America v. Kermit Warren*, Case No. 2:21-cv-1621 (S.D. Ohio 2021).

38. Sallah et al., "Stop and Seize."

39. Financial surveillance through KYC, AML, and CFT compliance has proved both ineffective and costly in practice. The U.S. government has long refused to provide data on the effectiveness of financial surveillance, and data on the costs of compliance suggest that the U.S. financial institutions spend approximately $46 billion a year. However, even if data could eventually prove that this regime has been effective at helping catch criminals from a cost–benefit perspective, that does not change the fundamental issue that requiring financial institutions to report private financial information without so much as a crime occurring runs counter to the spirit of the Fourth Amendment. For additional details in the context of how a CBDC would affect financial surveillance, see Chapter 4. For additional details about the U.S. financial surveillance regime in general, see Norbert Michel and Jennifer J. Schulp, "Revising the Bank Secrecy Act to Protect Privacy and Deter Criminals," Cato Institute Policy Analysis no. 932, July 26, 2022; Anthony, "The Right to Financial Privacy."

40. Anthony, "What Does Financial Privacy Mean for Liberty?"

41. Again, as Chris Meserole of the Brookings Institution correctly cautioned, it would likely take only a single event or set of events to lead officials toward abusing the powers that a CBDC system would make possible. *Bitcoin Magazine*, "Strategic Competition & Digital Currencies," YouTube video, September 27, 2023.

Chapter 6

1. F. A. Hayek, *The Road to Serfdom: The Definitive Edition*, ed. Bruce Caldwell (Chicago: University of Chicago Press, 2007), p. 79.

2. William J. Luther, "The CBDC Tradeoff," American Institute for Economic Research, October 9, 2022.

3. Luther, "The CBDC Tradeoff."

4. The risk of bank disintermediation is discussed in George Selgin, "Central Bank Digital Currency as a Potential Source of

Financial Instability," *Cato Journal* 41, no. 2 (2021): 333–41; Board of Governors of the Federal Reserve System, "Money and Payments: The U.S. Dollar in the Age of Digital Transformation," January 2022; Nicholas Anthony, "Public Comment Re: Central Bank Digital Currency," Cato Institute, May 12, 2022; Luther, "The CBDC Tradeoff"; Julia Weismann Seixas, Samuel Eddie Mogensen, and Søren Truels Nielsen, "New Types of Digital Money," Danmarks Nationalbank, June 23, 2022.

5. To make a CBDC more attractive than existing money, some have proposed paying interest, offering lotteries that only pay in CBDC, giving preferred tax status to CBDC payments, and the like.

6. Megan Greene, "Central Banks Need to Go Slow on Digital Currencies," *Financial Times*, August 26, 2021.

7. Emily Ekins and Jordan Gygi, "Poll: Only 16% of Americans Support the Government Issuing a Central Bank Digital Currency," Cato Institute, May 31, 2023; Stephen Deane and Oliver Fines, "CFA Institute Global Survey on Central Bank Digital Currencies," CFA Institute, July 2023.

8. Jamaica has also resorted to paying people to open accounts, and China has given away CBDCs via a lottery system. Although similarly troublesome, these tactics are not discussed at length because they are likely to encourage individuals to open an account for the initial payoff, but not lead to long-term use. Josimar Scott, "Digital Marketplace for Jam-Dex," *Jamaica Observer*, May 6, 2023; Nicholas Anthony, "Nigeria's CBDC Was Not Chosen. It Was Forced," *Cato at Liberty* (blog), Cato Institute, May 15, 2023.

9. Morgan Ricks, professor of law, Vanderbilt University Law School, Testimony before the Task Force on Financial Technology of the House Committee on Financial Services, 116th Cong., 2nd sess., June 11, 2020; Richard Turrin, *Cashless: China's Digital Currency Revolution* (Gold River, CA: Authority Publishing, 2021).

10. "Money and Payments," Board of Governors of the Federal Reserve System.

11. Seixas, Mogensen, and Nielsen, "New Types of Digital Money," p. 26.

12. Bernie Sanders, "Credit card interest rates are outrageously high. With @RepAOC, we are introducing legislation to challenge the greed of Wall Street and protect consumers across America," Periscope post, May 9, 2019.

13. Joshua R. Hendrickson, "Who Is Going to Use CBDCs?," *National Review*, October 19, 2022.

14. Hendrickson, "Who Is Going to Use CBDCs?"; Matt Levine, "Fed Rejects Bank for Being Too Safe," Bloomberg, September 6, 2018; John H. Cochrane, "The Safest Bank the Fed Won't Sanction," *Chicago Booth Review*, November 30, 2018.

15. E. W. Kemmerer, "The United States Postal Savings Bank," *Political Science Quarterly* 26, no. 3 (1911): 465.

16. Economists Matthew Jaremski, Sebastian Fleitas, and Steven Sprick Schuster report that during the 1930s, the relatively high, bureaucratically set rates on postal savings accounts "drew desperately needed funds away from private lenders, prolonging the effects of the Depression." Matthew Jaremski, Sebastian Fleitas, and Steven Sprick Schuster, "The US Postal Savings System and the Collapse of Building and Loan Associations during the Great Depression," Center for Growth and Opportunity at Utah State University Working Paper no. 2020.005, April 30, 2020, Executive Summary; James M. Boughton and Elmus R. Wicker, "The Behavior of the Currency-Deposit Ratio during the Great Depression," *Journal of Money, Credit and Banking* 11, no. 4 (1979): 405–18.

17. Kemmerer, "The United States Postal Savings Bank"; Lee K. Davison and Carlos D. Ramirez, "Does Deposit Insurance Promote Financial Depth? Evidence from the Postal Savings System during the 1920s," FDIC Center for Financial Research Working Paper no. 2017-02, November 2016.

18. For more on the history of the U.S. Postal Savings System, see Kemmerer, "The United States Postal Savings Bank"; "The Postal Savings System in the United States," 1937; Maureen O'Hara and David Easley, "The Postal Savings System in the Depression," *Journal of Economic History* 39, no. 3 (1979): 741–53.

19. For some CBDC proponents, however, crowding out private-sector alternatives is a feature, not a bug. When weighing the costs and benefits, CBDC consultant Richard Turrin said that

disrupting the banking system is the number one advantage of creating a CBDC, even though doing so would lead to "profound systemic changes that threaten entire lines of business within banks and credit card companies." Turrin, *Cashless: China's Digital Currency Revolution*.

20. Board of Governors of the Federal Reserve System, "Money and Payments"; Seraina Grünewald, "A Legal Framework for the Digital Euro: An Assessment of the ECB's First Three Progress Reports," European Parliament Think Tank In-Depth Analysis no. PE 741.518, May 2023.

21. Luther, "The CBDC Tradeoff."

22. Juda Agung, assistant governor of the Central Bank of Indonesia, said, "A CBDC would be one of the tools to fight crypto." Arys Aditya, "Bank Indonesia Mulls Digital Currency as a Way to 'Fight' Crypto," Bloomberg, November 30, 2021. In the *Financial Times*, Martin Wolf writes: "How should central banks respond to digital technology? This has become an urgent question. The answer is partly that both they and governments have to get a grip on the new wild west of private money. But it is also that they must now introduce digital currencies of their own." Martin Wolf, "The Time to Embrace Central Bank Digital Currencies Is Now," *Financial Times*, July 20, 2021.

23. Andrey Sergeenkov, "China Crypto Bans: A Complete History," CoinDesk, September 29, 2021.

24. The 2021 bill seeking to ban cryptocurrency and create a CBDC in India did not pass at the time, but its current status is unclear. Although the Indian government has launched a CBDC, it is still working on cryptocurrency legislation. What is to come is still to be seen, but recent statements from officials do not bode well. For instance, Reserve Bank of India governor Shaktikanta Das said in 2023 that "crypto should be banned" and Reserve Bank of India deputy governor T. Rabi Sankar recommended "putting as much effort as possible into ensuring that most digital currency usage [is] restricted to fiat currencies." Nidhi Bhardwaj, "RBI Gov Calls for an Outright Ban on Cryptocurrency as Union Budget 2023 Approaches," *India Today*, January 16, 2023; Human Rights Foundation's CBDC Tracker; Nicholas Anthony,

"India Seeks to Criminalize Cryptocurrencies," Foundation for Economic Education, March, 26, 2021.

25. Sebastian Sinclair, "Nigeria's Central Bank: We Didn't Ban Crypto Trading," CoinDesk, March 22, 2021.

26. Rep. Brad Sherman (D-CA), "Statement of Congressman Brad Sherman on Facebook Cryptocurrency Plan," Office of Representative Sherman press release, June 18, 2019.

27. Sen. Sherrod Brown (D-OH), "Brown Statement on Payment Providers Declining to Join Facebook's Libra Association," Senate Minority press release, October 11, 2019.

28. Rep. Jesús García (D-IL), H.R. 4813, Keep Big Tech Out of Finance Act, November 13, 2019.

29. Sen. Mike Crapo (R-ID), "Crapo Statement at Digital Currency Hearing," Senate Majority press release, June 30, 2020.

30. Zachary Warmbrodt, "Fear of Facebook Spurs Momentum for Fed to Build Its Own Digital Currency," *Politico*, October 15, 2019.

31. Warmbrodt, "Fear of Facebook Spurs Momentum for Fed."

32. House Committee on Financial Services, *Consumers First: Semi-Annual Report of the Consumer Financial Protection Bureau*, H. R. no. 117-110, 117th Cong., 2nd sess., 2022; GOP Financial Services, "Hill Delivers Remarks at Hearing on the Biden Administration's Attack on the Digital Asset Ecosystem," YouTube video, March 9, 2023.

33. Some commentators have described the video of Christine Lagarde as fake. Lagarde's comments are genuine. The "fake factor" is due to Lagarde's having been tricked by comedy duo Vladimir Krasnov and Aleksei Stolyarov into the interview. Lagarde thought she was talking to Ukraine president Volodymyr Zelensky. The duo has performed similar pranks on other notable figures as well. "ECB's Lagarde Gets Pranked, Reveals Digital Euro Will Have 'Limited' Control," Yahoo! Finance, April 7, 2023; PM News, "European Central Bank (ECB) President Christine Lagarde Recently Fell Victim to a Prank," YouTube video, May 17, 2023; Tobias Burns, "Fed Chief Duped into Fake Interview with Russians Posing as Zelensky," *The Hill*, April 27, 2023.

34. Luther, "The CBDC Tradeoff."

Chapter 7

1. David Z. Morris, "What If Somebody Hacks the Money Pipeline Next?," CoinDesk, May 13, 2021.

2. This sentence refers to the words "central," "bank," "digital," and "currency" as separate concepts.

3. Hacking attempts can include distributed denial-of-service attacks, advanced persistent threat attacks, malware attacks, social engineering attacks, user vulnerability attacks, malicious end user attacks, insider attacks, and more. Outages, on the other hand, could be caused by human error, natural disasters, technology failures, and obsolete technology. Bank for International Settlements, *Project Polaris: A Security and Resilience Framework for CBDC Systems* (Basel: BIS Innovation Hub, 2023).

4. Lael Brainard, "Cryptocurrencies, Digital Currencies, and Distributed Ledger Technologies: What Are We Learning?" (speech, Decoding Digital Currency Conference, San Francisco, CA, May 15, 2018). Oddly, in that same year, Martin Sandbu argued in the *Financial Times* that a disruption of Visa's payment network was a reason to introduce a CBDC. As my colleague, George Selgin, explained at the time: "Payments systems operated by central banks are similarly dependent on computer hardware and software, and are for that reason also vulnerable to both hacking and equipment failures. That's the first—and far from trivial—flaw in Sandbu's argument. Within the last two years, for example, hackers have used malware to steal millions from the central banks of Russia and Bangladesh. In the latter case the money came straight out of the Bangladesh Bank's account at the New York Fed." Martin Sandbu, "Visa Glitch Shows It Is High Time for Digital Cash," *Financial Times*, June 4, 2018; George Selgin, "The Computer-Glitch Argument for Central Bank eCash," *Alt-M* (blog), June 7, 2018.

5. Bank for International Settlements, *Project Polaris*, p. 12.

6. In addition to the issues experienced by U.S. financial regulators mentioned in this chapter, there have also been notable breaches and hacks in other U.S. government agencies. For example, the personal information of more than 22 million people was

exposed during two breaches, in 2014 and 2015, at the Office of Personnel Management. More recently, in 2023, the personal information of 237,000 current and former federal government employees was exposed in a breach at the U.S. Transportation Department. David Shepardson, "Data of 237,000 U.S. Government Employees Breached," Reuters, May 15, 2023.

7. Katy O'Donnell, "CFPB Says Employee Breached Data of 250,000 Consumers in 'Major Incident,'" *Politico*, April 19, 2023.

8. O'Donnell, "Employee Breached Data of 250,000 Consumers."

9. Kyle Campbell, "Senate Banking Republicans Want Answers from Fed on CSI Leak," *American Banker*, October 10, 2023.

10. Nathan Lynch and Brett Wolf, "U.S. FinCEN Leaks to Have 'Chilling Effect' on Fight against Financial Crime, Say AML Experts," Thomson Reuters, September 18, 2020; "FinCEN Files," International Consortium of Investigative Journalists, last updated July 20, 2023.

11. Dave Michaels, "SEC Discloses Edgar Corporate Filing System Was Hacked in 2016," *Wall Street Journal*, September 20, 2017.

12. Michael Corkery, "Hackers' $81 Million Sneak Attack on World Banking," *New York Times*, April 30, 2016; Krishna N. Das and Jonathan Spicer, "How the New York Fed Fumbled over the Bangladesh Bank Cyber-Heist," Reuters, July 21, 2016.

13. Joe Davidson, "'Inadvertent' Cyber Breach Hits 44,000 FDIC Customers," *Washington Post*, April 11, 2016.

14. Donna Borak, "U.S. Bank Regulator Notifies Congress of Major Data Security Breach," *Wall Street Journal*, October 28, 2016.

15. Jason Lange and Dustin Volz, "Exclusive: Fed Records Show Dozens of Cybersecurity Breaches," Reuters, June 1, 2016.

16. Richard Console Jr., "M&T Bank Files Notice of Data Breach Affecting Over 95K Massachusetts Residents," JD Supra, August 16, 2023; Niket Nishant and Lananh Nguyen, "JPMorgan Says It Is Not Seeing Any Impact from Alleged Hack," Reuters, October 11, 2022; "Citibank Confirms Hacking Attack," BBC, June 9, 2011.

17. "Bank of America Clients' 1 Billion Digital Logins in July Mark the Highest Month Ever," press release, Bank of America, August 25, 2022.

18. Corkery, "Hackers' $81 Million Sneak Attack"; Das and Spicer, "New York Fed Fumbled over the Bangladesh Bank Cyber-Heist."

19. There are cases where an individual might fall victim to a hack. However, the present discussion is focused on system-wide vulnerabilities of the network as a whole.

20. For additional information on 51 percent attacks, see Griffin Mcshane, "What Is a 51% Attack?," CoinDesk, October 12, 2021.

21. In 2022, the United States was the world leader in bitcoin mining. However, even then, all of the mining operations in the United States added up to only about 37 percent of global mining power. "Distribution of Bitcoin Mining Hashrate from September 2019 to January 2022, by Country," Statista, accessed September 2023.

22. For additional information on what it means to fork a system, see Arthur Cole, "Blockchain Fork," Techopedia, November 24, 2023.

23. As a general rule, incurring the wrath of the U.S. government is ill advised.

24. These data points were collected on August 29, 2023. "Today's Cryptocurrency Prices by Market Cap," CoinMarketCap, last updated August 28, 2023; "Monetary base; Total," Federal Reserve Economic Data (FRED), Federal Reserve Bank of St. Louis, last updated March 26, 2024.

25. Bank for International Settlements, *Project Polaris*.

26. Bank for International Settlements, *Project Polaris*.

27. Kate Davidson, "China Targets Fed to Gain Influence, Senator Charges, Drawing Powell Rebuke," *Politico*, July 26, 2022; Senate Committee on Homeland Security and Governmental Affairs, "China's Threat to the Fed: Chinese Influence and Information Theft at U.S. Federal Reserve Banks," Minority staff report, July 2022.

28. Davidson, "China Targets Fed"; Senate Committee on Homeland Security and Governmental Affairs, "Widespread Coverage Highlights Portman Report Detailing China's Efforts to Target, Influence, and Undermine U.S. Federal Reserve," Minority news, July 28, 2022.

29. Michael S. Derby, "A Year after Trading Scandal, Fed Is Again under Ethics Spotlight," Reuters, November 1, 2022; Sen. Elizabeth Warren (D-MA), letter to Jerome Powell, chair of the Board of Governors of the Federal Reserve System, August 11, 2022.

30. These policy decisions are made by the Federal Open Market Committee every six weeks or so.

31. Derby, "Fed Is Again under Ethics Spotlight."

32. The Eastern Caribbean Central Bank oversees the Eastern Caribbean Currency Union. Members of the currency union include Anguilla, Antigua and Barbuda, Dominica, Grenada, Montserrat, Saint Kitts and Nevis, Saint Lucia, and Saint Vincent and the Grenadines. At the time of this writing, the post is not available on the Eastern Caribbean Central Bank's website. Luckily, it had been logged on the internet archive. "Region-Wide Service Interruption of DCash Platform," Eastern Caribbean Central Bank, January 14, 2022.

33. Jim Wyss, "A Bold Caribbean Experiment in E-Cash Hits a Major Obstacle," Bloomberg, February 21, 2022.

34. Brooke Crothers, "Digital Currency Hit by Expired Certificate—Root Cause for Prolonged Outage," *Venafi* (blog), March 17, 2022.

35. Much like Note 32, the post is no longer available on the Eastern Caribbean Central Bank's website. Luckily, it had been logged on the internet archive. "DCash Service Resumes," Eastern Caribbean Central Bank, March 9, 2022; David B. Black, "DCash Shows Why Fedcoin Could Be a Disaster," *Forbes*, February 28, 2022.

36. Matt Egan, "The Federal Reserve Suffers Widespread Disruption to Payment Services," CNN Business, February 25, 2021.

37. Egan, "Federal Reserve Suffers Widespread Disruption."

Chapter 8

1. Christina Parajon Skinner, assistant professor of legal studies and business ethics, Wharton School of the University of Pennsylvania, "Digital Dollar Dilemma: The Implications of a Central Bank Digital Currency and Private Sector Alternatives," Testimony before the Subcommittee on Digital Assets, Financial Technology, and Inclusion of the House Committee on Financial Services, 118th Cong., 1st sess., September 14, 2023, p. 4.

2. Credit goes to David Beckworth, host of the *Macro Musings Podcast*, for encouraging this chapter. David Beckworth, "Nicholas Anthony on the Current Prospects and Legislative Developments Surrounding CBDC," *Macro Musings Podcast*, September 4, 2023.

3. Board of Governors of the Federal Reserve System, "Careers at the Federal Reserve Board"; Board of Governors of the Federal Reserve System, *109th Annual Report of the Board of Governors of the Federal Reserve System*, Report to Congress (Washington: Board of Governors, Federal Reserve System, 2022).

4. In fact, the Federal Reserve is so large that it may be due for cutbacks.

5. Board of Governors of the Federal Reserve System, "Careers at the Federal Reserve Board"; Board of Governors of the Federal Reserve System, *109th Annual Report*; Office of Personnel Management, "Federal Agencies List," Open Government Data, U.S. Office of Personnel Management; Bank of America, *Annual Report 2022* (Charlotte, NC: Bank of America, 2022); "Number of Employees at Wells Fargo from 2009 to 2023," Statista; "Number of Employees of JPMorgan Chase from 2008 to 2022," Statista.

6. Megan Greene, "Central Banks Need to Go Slow on Digital Currencies," *Financial Times*, August 26, 2021.

7. "Concept Note on Central Bank Digital Currency," Reports, Reserve Bank of India, October 7, 2022.

8. "True Cost of Financial Crime Compliance Study 2023: U.S. & Canada," LexisNexis Risk Solutions, 2022.

9. Credit goes to Lawrence White of George Mason University for pointing out these factors when describing the Ecuadorian

experience in 2014. As he notes, "The Ecuadorian case also shows that implementation of a central bank electronic money system isn't so easy." Lawrence H. White, "The World's First Central Bank Electronic Money Has Come—And Gone: Ecuador, 2014–2018," *Cato at Liberty* (blog), Cato Institute, April 2, 2018.

10. White, "First Central Bank Electronic Money Has Come—and Gone."

11. As noted by Rep. Brad Sherman (D-CA) at a congressional hearing considering CBDCs, "Let's point out that the Fed is really bad at retail." House Committee on Financial Services, "Digital Dollar Dilemma: The Implications of a Central Bank Digital Currency and . . . (EventID=116340)," YouTube video, September 14, 2023; White, "First Central Bank Electronic Money Has Come—And Gone."

12. Claire Kopsky, "Staffing Shortages Lead to Long DMV Wait Times," WBTV (Charlotte, NC), July 12, 2023; Jesal Dalal et al., "The Call to Rethink Government Customer Experience," McKinsey & Company, July 28, 2022.

13. Joseph R. Biden Jr., "Executive Order on Transforming Federal Customer Experience and Service Delivery to Rebuild Trust in Government," White House, December 13, 2021.

14. Chris Edwards, "Why the Federal Government Fails," Cato Institute Policy Analysis no. 777, July 27, 2015.

15. University of Auckland, Website Video Repository, "The Rise of Central Bank Digital Currencies—Barry Eichengreen," YouTube video, November 25, 2021.

16. "Does the U.S. Need a National Digital Currency?," *Wall Street Journal*, February 23, 2020.

17. Tobias Adrian, "Evolving to Work Better Together: Public-Private Partnerships for Digital Payments" (speech, Building CBDC: A Race to Reality Conference, sponsored by R3, Washington, July 22, 2020); Sandra Waliczek and Arushi Goel, "When It Comes to CBDCs, We Need Public-Private Cooperation," World Economic Forum, May 23, 2022; Burkhard Balz, "Public-Private Partnership—Key to the Success of a Digital Euro" (speech, Bitkom Digital Euro Summit (virtual), November 16, 2022).

18. "CBN Selects Technical Partner for Digital Currency Project," Central Bank of Nigeria press release, August 30, 2021.

19. Dipo Olowookere, "eNaira App Pulled Down from Google Play Store after Bad Reviews," *Business Post*, October 27, 2021.

20. Anthony Osae-Brown, Emele Onu, and Anna Irrera, "Nigeria Seeks Partners for Tech Revamp of Its eNaira Digital Currency," Bloomberg, February 21, 2023.

21. Notably, the same company (Bitt Inc.) worked on the CBDC for the Eastern Caribbean and Nigeria. Central Bank of Nigeria, "CBN Selects Technical Partner for Digital Currency Project."

22. For example, Columbia Business School finance professor Charles Calomiris has noted that previous expansions of the Federal Reserve's regulatory and supervisory authority via the Gramm-Leach-Bliley Act of 1999 and the Dodd-Frank Act of 2010 have already "made the central bank a party to new political bargains." Charles W. Calomiris, "Central Bankers in Glass Houses," *Wall Street Journal*, August 15, 2019; Charles I. Plosser, "Fiscal Policy and Monetary Policy—Restoring the Boundaries" (speech, U.S. Monetary Policy Forum, University of Chicago Booth School of Business, New York, NY, February 24, 2012).

23. Paul Volcker et al., "America Needs an Independent Fed," *Wall Street Journal*, August 5, 2019.

24. For example, one of the recommendations at the end of this book is to establish fixed criteria and third-party audits for when the Federal Reserve proposes market interventions under the Depository Institutions Deregulation and Monetary Control Act of 1980. Mark Calabria, "If Anyone Needs an Audit, It's the Federal Reserve," *The Hill*, February 3, 2015; Calomiris, "Central Bankers in Glass Houses."

25. James A. Dorn, "Why the Fed Needs a Monetary Rule to Protect Its Independence," *Alt-M* (blog), September 4, 2019; George Selgin, *The Menace of Fiscal QE* (Washington: Cato Institute, 2020).

26. Dorn, "Why the Fed Needs a Monetary Rule."

27. The legislative markup covered the following acts: Power of the Mint Act, CBDC Anti-Surveillance State Act, Agricultural

Security Risk Review Act, Safeguarding American Farms from Foreign Influence Act, Chinese Military and Surveillance Company Sanctions Act, FinCEN Oversight and Accountability Act of 2023, Financial Privacy Act of 2023, Protect Small Business and Prevent Illicit Financial Activity Act, Combatting Foreign Surveillance Spyware Sanctions Act, Financial Access Improvements Act, Russia and Belarus Financial Sanctions Act of 2023, and Foreign Affiliates Sharing Pilot Program Extension Act. Of these bills, the first two were written to prevent the issuance of a U.S. CBDC. GOP Financial Services, "Markup of Various Measures," YouTube video, September 20, 2023.

28. Calomiris, "Central Bankers in Glass Houses."

29. Credit goes to Norbert Michel of the Cato Institute for highlighting these examples during a congressional hearing. House Committee on Financial Services, Hearing on the "Digital Dollar Dilemma: The Implications of a Central Bank Digital Currency and . . . (EventID=116340)," YouTube video, September 14, 2023.

30. Bank for International Settlements Innovation Hub, *Project Polaris: A Security and Resilience Framework for CBDC Systems* (Basel: BIS Innovation Hub, 2023).

31. George Selgin, William D. Lastrapes, and Lawrence H. White, "Has the Fed Been a Failure?," *Journal of Macroeconomics* 34, no. 3 (2012): 569–96.

32. Volcker et al., "America Needs an Independent Fed."

33. Alberto Alesina and Lawrence H. Summers, "Central Bank Independence and Macroeconomic Performance: Some Comparative Evidence," *Journal of Money, Credit and Banking* 25, no. 2 (1993): 151–62; Ana Carolina Garriga, "Central Bank Independence in the World: A New Dataset," *International Interactions* 42, no. 5 (2016): 849–68; Carola Conces Binder, "Political Pressure on Central Banks," *Journal of Money, Credit and Banking* 53, no. 4 (June 2021): 715–44; Finn E. Kydland and Edward C. Prescott, "Rules Rather than Discretion: The Inconsistency of Optimal Plans," *Journal of Political Economy* 85, no. 3 (June 1977): 473–92.

34. "The Public's Trust Is the Fed's Most Important Asset, Says Fed Chair Powell," CNBC, November 2, 2022.

35. For the record, I see nothing wrong with questioning the status quo. However, I'd rather people do so because competition has made better options available and not because a monopoly has failed. For examples of recent polling, see James Diamond and Johnny Sawyer, "Few Americans Understand the Federal Reserve's Role Outside Curbing Inflation," Ipsos, April 30, 2022; Karlyn Bowman, "The Fed and Public Opinion," *Forbes*, May 9, 2023.

36. Plosser, "Fiscal Policy and Monetary Policy," p. 3.

37. Plosser, "Fiscal Policy and Monetary Policy," p. 3.

38. Plosser, "Fiscal Policy and Monetary Policy."

39. Calomiris, "Central Bankers in Glass Houses."

40. Calomiris, "Central Bankers in Glass Houses."

Chapter 9

1. Emily Ekins and Jordan Gygi, "Poll: Only 16% of Americans Support the Government Issuing a Central Bank Digital Currency," Cato Institute, May 31, 2023.

2. Stephen Deane and Oliver Fines, "CFA Institute Global Survey on Central Bank Digital Currencies," CFA Institute, July 2023.

3. Reps. Tom Emmer (R-MN), Jake Auchincloss (D-MA), and Alex X. Mooney (R-WV) have introduced legislation in the House, and Sens. Mike Lee (R-UT) and Ted Cruz (R-TX) have introduced legislation in the Senate. Nicholas Anthony, "CBDC Legislation Recap," *Cato at Liberty* (blog), Cato Institute, July 6, 2023.

4. Norbert Michel and Jennifer J. Schulp, "Revising the Bank Secrecy Act to Protect Privacy and Deter Criminals," Cato Institute Policy Analysis no. 932, July 26, 2022; Nicholas Anthony, "The Right to Financial Privacy: Crafting a Better Framework for Financial Privacy in the Digital Age," Cato Institute Policy Analysis no. 945, May 2, 2023.

5. *United States v. Jones*, 565 U.S. 400 (2012).

6. Nicholas Anthony, "Congress Should Welcome Cryptocurrency Competition," Cato Institute Briefing Paper no. 138, May 2, 2022; Anthony, "The Right to Financial Privacy."

Appendix B

1. This language is modified from the work of Rep. Tom Emmer (R–MN), Sen. Ted Cruz (R–TX), and Sen. Mike Lee (R–UT). "Emmer Introduces Legislation to Prevent Unilateral Fed Control of a U.S. Digital Currency," press release, Office of Representative Emmer, January 12, 2022; "Sen. Cruz Introduces Legislation Prohibiting Unilateral Fed Control of a U.S. Digital Currency," press release, Office of Senator Cruz, March 30, 2022; "Senator Lee Introduces the No CBDC Act," press release, Office of Senator Lee, September 14, 2022.

2. Barack Obama, "Retirement Savings Security," 79 Fed. Reg. 6455, February 4, 2014; Robert Hockett, "Digital Greenbacks," *Forbes*, May 17, 2020.

3. Bureau of the Fiscal Service, Direct Express website.

4. George Selgin, director, Cato Institute Center for Monetary and Financial Alternatives, "Facilitating Faster Payments in the U.S.," Testimony before the Senate Committee on Banking, Housing, and Urban Affairs, 116th Cong., 1st sess., September 25, 2019.

5. Board of Governors of the Federal Reserve System, "Notification of 2024 Private Sector Adjustment Factor and Fee Schedules," Federal Reserve System Docket No. OP-1822.

6. Selgin, "Facilitating Faster Payments in the U.S."

7. Selgin, "Facilitating Faster Payments in the U.S."

8. Norbert Michel and Jennifer J. Schulp, "Revising the Bank Secrecy Act to Protect Privacy and Deter Criminals," Cato Institute Policy Analysis no. 932, July 26, 2022.

9. This language is slightly modified from the Counter Terrorism and Illicit Finance Act. House Committee on Financial Services, Counter Terrorism and Illicit Finance Act, 115th Cong., 2nd sess., Report no. 1156068, 2018.

10. This language is slightly modified from the Financial Crimes Enforcement Network Improvement Act and the National Defense Authorization Act for Fiscal Year 2021. House Committee on Financial Services, Financial Crimes Enforcement Network Improvement Act, 117th Cong., 2nd sess.,

Report no. 1177623, 2022; House Committee on Armed Services, William M. (Mac) Thornberry National Defense Authorization Act for Fiscal Year 2021, 116th Cong., 2nd sess., Report no. 1166395, 2021.

11. Nicholas Anthony, "The Infrastructure Investment and Jobs Act's Attack on Crypto: Questioning the Rationale for the Cryptocurrency Provisions," Cato Institute Briefing Paper no. 129, November 15, 2021; Abraham Sutherland, *Research Report on Tax Code Section 6050I and Digital Assets* (New York: Proof of Stake Alliance, 2021).

12. Nicholas Anthony and Ivane Nachkebia, "How the Market, Not Government, Regulates Cryptocurrency Crimes," *Cato at Liberty* (blog), Cato Institute, August 23, 2022. For example, two Chinese intelligence officers attempted to bribe a U.S. government employee with bitcoins, but the use of cryptocurrency did little to halt their identification. "Two Chinese Intelligence Officers Charged with Obstruction of Justice in Scheme to Bribe U.S. Government Employee and Steal Documents Related to the Federal Prosecution of a PRC-Based Company," Department of Justice press release, October 24, 2022; Nicholas Anthony, "Reporting FinCEN's Suspicious Activity," *Cato at Liberty* (blog), Cato Institute, April 13, 2022; Nicholas Anthony, "Stop Deputizing Banks as Law Enforcement Agents," *Cato at Liberty* (blog), Cato Institute, May 3, 2022; Nicholas Anthony, policy analyst, Cato Institute Center for Monetary and Financial Alternatives, "Oversight of the Financial Crimes Enforcement Network," Testimony before the House Committee on Financial Services, 117th Cong., 2nd sess., April 28, 2022.

13. This language is slightly modified from the Keep Your Coins Act. House Committee on Financial Services, Keep Your Coins Act, 117th Cong., 2nd sess., Report no. 1176727, 2022.

14. Internal Revenue Service, "Schedule D, Form 1040."

15. Neeraj Agrawal, "Congress Takes a Step toward a De Minimis Exemption for Everyday Cryptocurrency Transactions," Coin Center, February 3, 2022; Rep. Suzan DelBene (D-WA), "DelBene, Schweikert Introduce Bipartisan Legislation to Expand Use of Virtual Currency," press release, Office of Representative DelBene, February 3, 2022.

Appendix C

1. Norbert Michel and Nicholas Anthony, "The Risks of CBDCs: Why Central Bank Digital Currencies Shouldn't Be Adopted," Cato Institute, February 22, 2023.

2. Cato Institute, "39th Annual Monetary Conference: Populism and the Future of the Fed," YouTube video, November 18, 2021.

3. Lawrence H. White (@lawrencehwhite1), "You don't have to be a fan of the banking system status quo to see the surveillance danger in CBDC," X, October 9, 2021, 9:03 a.m.; Richard Yan, Robert Hockett, and Lawrence White, "Motion: The US Urgently Needs to Catch Up on Central Bank Digital Currency (Robert Hockett vs. Lawrence White)," *The Blockchain Debate Podcast*, June 18, 2021.

4. Christina Parajon Skinner, assistant professor of legal studies and business ethics, Wharton School of the University of Pennsylvania, "Digital Dollar Dilemma: The Implications of a Central Bank Digital Currency and Private Sector Alternatives," Testimony before the Subcommittee on Digital Assets, Financial Technology, and Inclusion of the House Committee on Financial Services, 118th Cong., 1st sess., September 14, 2023, p. 12.

5. William J. Luther, "Will a Digital Dollar Offer Financial Privacy?," American Institute for Economic Research, October 7, 2022.

6. Barry Eichengreen, "CBDCs Still Have Not Found Their Raison d'Être," *Financial Times*, December 5, 2023.

7. Patrick Schueffel, "CBDCs: Pros and Cons—A Comprehensive List and Discussion of the Advantages and Disadvantages of Central Bank Digital Currency," *Journal of Digital Assets* 1, no. 2 (2023): 54.

8. Christos Makridis, "Are CBDCs Kryptonite for Crypto?," *Cointelegraph*, April 6, 2022.

9. Richard Epstein and Max Raskin, "CBDCs Wrongfully Break Down the Separation between Money and State," CoinDesk, July 27, 2023.

10. Martin Arnold and Sam Fleming, "The Digital Euro: A Solution Seeking a Problem?," *Financial Times*, May 16, 2023.

11. Norbert Michel, "CBDCs Are Bigger than Politics," *Forbes*, April 18, 2023.

12. Ryan Bourne, "Why Sunak Should Think Twice about a Central Bank Digital Currency," *Conservative Home* (blog), November 17, 2021.

13. Gina Heeb, "A Digital Dollar for the Unbanked? Banks, Consumers See Pitfalls," *Bloomberg Law*, June 22, 2022.

14. *Bitcoin Magazine*, "Strategic Competition & Digital Currencies," YouTube video, September 27, 2023.

15. David Waugh, "Fed's Cryptocurrency Pilot Opens Door for Dangerous Retail Option," *The Hill*, December 8, 2022.

16. Natalie Smolenski and Dan Held, "Why the U.S. Should Reject Central Bank Digital Currencies (CBDCs)," Bitcoin Policy Institute, September 27, 2022, p. 12.

17. Alex Gladstein, "Financial Freedom and Privacy in the Post-Cash World," *Cato Journal* 41, no. 2 (2021): 283.

18. Quote provided in direct correspondence with the author.

19. "CBDCs Are 'A Disaster for Privacy': The Government Must Listen to Warnings from Around the World and Rethink the Digital Pound," Big Brother Watch, November 29, 2023.

20. The Federalist Society, "Central Bank Digital Currency—Efficient Innovation or the End of the Private Banking System?," YouTube video, May 18, 2022.

21. Ari Patinkin and John Berlau, "The Global Rejection of CBDCs," *Real Clear Markets*, August 3, 2023.

22. Michael Faulkender and David Vasquez, "Research Report: Central Bank Digital Currencies," America First Policy Institute, August 17, 2023, p. 12.

23. Quote provided in direct correspondence with the author.

24. Gregory Baer, "Central Bank Digital Currencies: Costs, Benefits and Major Implications for the U.S. Economic System," Bank Policy Institute staff working paper, April 7, 2021, p. 2.

25. Nicholas Anthony, "Update: Two Thirds of Commenters Concerned about CBDC," *Cato at Liberty* (blog), Cato Institute, July 27, 2022.

26. Rob Morgan, Letter to Ann E. Misback, secretary of the Board of Governors of the Federal Reserve System, "ABA

Comments on Federal Reserve Discussion Paper Money and Payments: The US Dollar in the Age of Digital Transformation," American Bankers Association, May 20, 2022, p. 1.

27. Deborah Matthews Phillips and Mickey Marshall, Letter to Ann E. Misback, secretary of the Board of Governors of the Federal Reserve System, "Request for Comment Regarding the Board of Governors of the Federal Reserve System Public Consultation Paper, *Money and Payments: The U.S. Dollar in the Age of Digital Transformation*," Independent Community Bankers of America, May 20, 2022, p. 1.

28. Sean Fieler, "A CBDC Dollar Would Empower the Fed, Not Americans," *Wall Street Journal*, February 7, 2023.

29. Dante Alighieri Disparte, "Is America Losing the Digital-Currency Race?," Project Syndicate, July 2, 2021.

30. Quote provided in direct correspondence with the author.

31. David Z. Morris, "What If Somebody Hacks the Money Pipeline Next?," CoinDesk, May 13, 2021.

32. Justin Amash (@justinamash), "Decentralize money. No digital dollar. A digital U.S. currency would be one of the most dangerous developments in history. When government can simply flip a switch to block all your transactions, it controls your entire life. We need a wall of separation between money and state," X, November 16, 2022, 11:36 a.m.

33. House Committee on Financial Services, "The Promises and Perils of Central Bank Digital Currencies (EventID=113989)," YouTube video, July 27, 2021.

34. Sam Sutton, "Banks, Crypto Lobby Clash with Lawmakers over Fed Digital Dollar," *Politico*, August 22, 2022.

35. House Committee on Financial Services, "Digital Assets and the Future of Finance: Examining the Benefits and Risks of a U.S. Central Bank Digital Currency (EventID=114689)," YouTube video, May 26, 2022.

36. Ted Cruz (@tedcruz), "Biden just released his crypto reg 'framework' encouraging the Fed to keep developing a CBDC, which the Fed Chair admits would destroy cryptocurrencies. A CBDC would allow the gov to spy on us. Congress needs to pass my bill that stops the Fed from developing a CBDC now!," X, September 16, 2022, 10:49 a.m.

37. Warren Davidson (@WarrenDavidson), "#SoundMoney is essential to defending freedom. As described here, by the UK's likely Prime Minister, CBDC is a corruption of money. A centrally managed, centrally controlled, Central Bank Digital Currency (CBDC) is a tool for coercion and control," X, October 24, 2022, 12:03 p.m.

38. Rep. Tom Emmer (R-MN), "Emmer Introduces Legislation to Prevent Unilateral Fed Control of a U.S. Digital Currency," Office of Representative Emmer press release, January 12, 2022.

39. GOP Financial Services, "Markup of Various Measures," YouTube video, September 20, 2023.

40. *Hearing on Digital Dollar Dilemma: The Implications of a Central Bank Digital Currency and Private Sector Alternatives, Before the Committee on Financial Services, Subcommittee on Digital Assets, Financial Technology, and Inclusion*, 118th Cong. 1st sess. (September 14, 2023).

41. Rep. Mark Green (@RepMarkGreen), "There's no question about it; CBDCs are about containment, surveillance, and control," X, August 7, 2023, 4:00 p.m.

42. Sen. Mike Lee (R-UT), "Sen. Lee Fights Central Bank Digital Currency," press release, Office of Senator Lee, March 24, 2023.

43. Rep. Patrick McHenry (R-NC), "McHenry Statement on Biden Administration's Digital Assets Reports," press release, House Financial Services Committee, September 16, 2022.

44. "Governor Ron DeSantis Announces Legislation to Protect Floridians from a Federally Controlled Central Bank Digital Currency and Surveillance State," news release, Office of Gov. Ron DeSantis, March 20, 2023.

45. Nicholas Anthony, "Chair Powell Chats CBDCs at Cato," *Cato at Liberty* (blog), Cato Institute, September 15, 2022.

46. Christopher J. Waller, "The U.S. Dollar and Central Bank Digital Currencies" (speech, Digital Currencies and National Security Tradeoffs Symposium, Cambridge, MA, October 14, 2022).

47. Neel Kashkari, "Fireside Chat at the 2022 Journal of Financial Regulation Conference," YouTube video, August 3, 2022.

48. Randal K. Quarles, "Parachute Pants and Central Bank Money" (speech, 113th Annual Utah Bankers Association Convention, Sun Valley, ID, June 28, 2021).

49. Felipe M. Medalla, "The Current Philippine Digital Landscape—What's Next beyond the Digital Payments Transformation Roadmap" (speech, FinTech Alliance.ph General Membership Meeting, Manila, May 29, 2023).

50. David Ljunggren, "Bank of Canada Not Planning to Launch Digital Currency, at Least for Now," Reuters, October 18, 2021.

51. Philip Lowe, "Payments: The Future?" (speech, Australian Payments Network Summit, online, December 9, 2021).

52. International Monetary Fund, "New Economy Forum: IMF Approach to Central Bank Digital Currency Capacity Development," April 12, 2023.

53. Joseph Wang, *Central Banking 101* (New York: Self-published, 2020).

INDEX

Note: Information in figures and tables is indicated by *f* and *t*; n designates a numbered note.

ABOUT THE AUTHOR

Nicholas Anthony is a policy analyst at the Cato Institute's Center for Monetary and Financial Alternatives and a fellow at the Human Rights Foundation (HRF). Anthony's research covers a wide range of topics within the field of monetary and financial economics, including central bank digital currency (CBDC), financial privacy, cryptocurrency, and the use of money in society. He has testified before Congress and his work has been published in the *Wall Street Journal*, *MarketWatch*, *Business Insider*, the American Institute for Economic Research, and numerous other outlets. Anthony also maintains the HRF CBDC Tracker, which documents CBDC development and civil liberties concerns around the world.

Originally from Baltimore, Anthony received a BS in economics and business administration from Towson University and an MA in economics from George Mason University.

ABOUT THE CATO INSTITUTE AND CENTER FOR MONETARY AND FINANCIAL ALTERNATIVES

Founded in 1977, the Cato Institute is a public policy research foundation dedicated to broadening the parameters of policy debate to allow consideration of more options that are consistent with the principles of limited government, individual liberty, and peace. The Institute is named for *Cato's Letters*, libertarian pamphlets that were widely read in the American colonies in the early 18th century and played a major role in laying the philosophical foundation for the American Revolution.

The Cato Institute undertakes an extensive publications program on the complete spectrum of policy issues. Books, monographs, and shorter studies are commissioned to examine the federal budget, Social Security, regulation, military spending, international trade, and myriad other issues. Major policy conferences are held throughout the year.

The Cato Institute's Center for Monetary and Financial Alternatives was founded in 2014 to assess the shortcomings of existing monetary and financial regulatory arrangements, and to discover and promote more stable and efficient alternatives.

In order to maintain its independence, the Cato Institute accepts no government funding. Contributions are received from foundations, corporations, and individuals, and other revenue is generated from the sale of publications. The Institute is a nonprofit, tax-exempt, educational foundation under Section 501(c)3 of the Internal Revenue Code.

CATO INSTITUTE
1000 Massachusetts Ave. NW
Washington, DC 20001
www.cato.org